Pub Walks
in Lancashire

Neil Coates

SIGMA LEISURE

Wilmslow, England

First published in 1991 by Sigma Leisure – an imprint of Sigma Press, 1 South Oak Lane, Wilmslow, Cheshire SK9 6AR, England.
Reprinted in 1991.

Whilst every effort has been made to ensure that the information given in this book is correct, neither the publisher nor the author accept any responsibility for any inaccuracy.

British Library Cataloguing in Publication Data
A CIP record for this book is available from the British Library.

ISBN: 1-85058-256-4

Typesetting and design by
Sigma Hi-Tech Services Ltd, Wilmslow

Printed and bound by
Manchester Free Press, Paragon Mill, Jersey St., Manchester M4 6FP.

Cover Picture: The sunlit forecourt of the Black Dog at Belmont, a welcome break for ramblers in the West Pennines *(Photograph: Clive Weake)*

PREFACE

Lancashire is both geographical area and state of mind. Those born in the Red Rose County are fiercely proud of the fact and generally choose to dissociate themselves from the foibles of latter-day local government eccentricities. After all, England's greatest cricketing side is still based at Old Trafford – could this be anything but in Lancashire? And the greatest football teams – can they logically be saddled with addresses in Greater Manchester or Merseyside? To all those of sound mind, Lancashire still stretches from the Mersey to the high peaks of the Lake District

This pride also extends to the countryside. Yet the County is only now coming into its own and being discovered, by both residents and visitors alike, as the very best of countryside walking areas. Geographically the County is one of the most diverse in Britain, from the eerie windswept marshes of the coast to the high moors of the Pennines, the craggy limestone country in the north to the lush, sinuous valleys of the Hodder, Ribble and Lune there's countryside for virtually all tastes. Even local ramblers are constantly amazed at new discoveries around every corner.

"Pub Walks in Lancashire" aims to share aspects of all these landscapes with you, with the additional bonanza of a few hours whiled away in convivial country hostelries. The walks themselves are not claimed to be necessarily the most scenic or challenging in the County, nor the pubs necessarily the best; obviously such things are purely subjective. I've sought to combine walks and pubs which should give you an excellent taste of that which Lancashire has to offer in terms of walking and of good beer; with some the pub was the prime mover and a walk fitted in around, with others the walk was the target. A good geographical spread was the aim, but I make no apologies for excluding town pubs and walks or some very well known countryside spots in the Lake District – there's another book's worth of these just itching to be researched.

Virtually all the walks are readily accessible on a regular basis by public transport from one or more of the main towns in Lancashire; where possible I've indicated in the titles of each walk the relevant rail service to use. For specific train times your local rail enquiry office (in the phone book) will advise. Bus services are generally too prone to changes to make detailing them here worthwhile; your best bet is to ring the very helpful County Council Transport Enquiry Service, telephone Preston (0772) 263333, for up to date information. If you're travelling by car then almost all the pubs featured have a dedicated car park where you can park up whilst you enjoy the walk, provided, of course, that you intend to use the pub before you set out or when you return breathless and thirsty; if you get the chance, have a word with the landlord before you set out. At the few which don't have a car park there's safe roadside parking or a village car park nearby.

Most of the research for this book was undertaken during the winter, an unbeatable time to walk when the sun is up and the ground crisp with frost or snow – but it can be atrociously muddy. My heartfelt thanks go to the landladies and landlords whose irrepressible forbearance at the sight of the author and companions tramping yet another field full of mud into their floor (despite valiant attempts to clean boots at the door) was matched by their knowledge of the pub's history, the local area and by their innkeeping skills.

Thanks also to my walking companions and route-testers, Bev Ridyard, Paul Richardson and Fred Laugharne, whose diligence in sampling bar meals and real ales proved formidable; to Clive Weake of the West Pennine Moors Ranger Service and Nick Osborne at the County Countryside Unit. Finally a particular expression of gratitude to Jenny and Terry Reilly for hospitality above and beyond the call of duty on numerous visits during the course of research.

Neil Coates

LOCATION MAP

CONTENTS

THE FYLDE

Location	Distance	Pub	
Wharles	7 miles	Eagle and Child	101
Glasson	7.5 miles	Stork Inn	108
Cuddy Hill	5 miles	Plough at Eaves	116

CENTRAL LANCASHIRE

Location	Distance	Pub	
Waddington	7 miles	Buck Inn	121
Goosnargh	5.5 miles	Grapes Inn	128
Holden	6 miles	Copy Nook Hotel	134
Ribchester	8 miles	White Bull	142

ROSSENDALE

Location	Distance	Pub	
Cowpe	8.5 miles	Buck	149
Nangreaves	7.5 miles	Lord Raglan	156
Mereclough	7 miles	Kettledrum	162

NORTH LUNE

Location	Distance	Pub	
Hornby	8 miles	Royal Oak	169
Overton	6.5 miles	Ship Hotel	176
Warton	7 miles	Black Bull	182

WHITHER LANCASHIRE?

As an entity, Lancashire goes back only to the Twelfth Century when the lands between the Mersey and Duddon rivers were first treated as one for Exchequer purposes and essentially controlled by one individual, John, Count of Mortain, later King John. The area's history is, of course, infinitely older: stone circles, cairns, hill forts and tumuli testify to pre-historic settlement; the Romans left a legacy of forts and roads; Scandinavian place names from the Eighth to Eleventh Centuries abound and there are records, albeit meagre, in the Domesday survey of 1086 (for the purposes of which lands south of the Ribble were counted as Cheshire and north of the Ribble as Yorkshire, perish the thought). A century after King John another John, the redoubtable John of Gaunt, established the County as a Palatinate, virtually a self-governing state within England with its own judicial system. Such powers continued for centuries afterwards in the guise of the Duchy of Lancaster; problems raised by this contributed to the Wars of the Roses in the Fifteenth Century.

From the Fifteenth to the Seventeenth Centuries Lancashire in most respects mirrored the development of much of the rest of England. The population grew steadily, if slowly, estimates suggest around 200,000 in 1690 of which perhaps one in six lived in towns. In the countryside a rich and diverse agricultural base developed which has left a strong legacy to this day. Catholicism remained the dominant religious trait, but with a strong Puritan element developing in the towns; this divide was reflected in the Civil War which proved largely town against country in the region. In one area, however, Lancashire differed from most of the rest of England. Few Guilds or Corporations gained precedence in the towns or countryside meaning that the County was essentially a free trade area where anyone could trade in anything without the necessity to make recourse to Guild membership or training. This was to have a profound effect on the County.

It was the Eighteenth and Nineteenth Centuries that saw the County rise to prominence thanks to the textile industries. The foundations of such were laid in those non-Guild days of the previous two centuries with the unfettered development of the linen industry on the coastal plain, the woollen industry in the rural West Pennine area and the fustian (a mixture of cotton with linen or wool) industry to the north of Manchester. It was this latter manufacture that led to the growth of the cotton industry – King Cotton – for which the County became world renowned. The inventive minds of Arkwright, Kay and Crompton nurtured the birth of the Industrial Revolution in Lancashire which was to sweep England to World dominance under Victoria, a dominance powered and funded largely by the north west. The period also saw the rapid development of the "Cotton Towns" and the growth of Manchester and Liverpool as major world cities. Other important industries developed in tandem with textiles – coal mining, heavy engineering, steelmaking and shipbuilding – but all are now largely poignant memories; the County has suffered more than most from the economic changes, traits and absurdities of the past thirty years.

Politics dealt Lancashire a severe blow in 1974 when the County was dismembered following the Maud Commission report. At a stroke the County "lost" Manchester and Liverpool, many of the cotton towns and a large chunk of southern Lakeland; the County boundary once ran up the middle of Windermere whilst Coniston Water was the County's largest lake. You'll find few supporters of this local government gerrymandering today, Mancunians and Liverpudlians alike remain staunchly Lancastrian. Conversely, the same changes saw Lancashire landed with parts of Yorkshire; large areas of Bowland changed from White to Red Rose overnight, a similar plight (sic) befell residents of Saddleworth, east of Oldham. Many of the good burghers in the communities north of Clitheroe still claim to be Yorkshire born and bred and, uniquely, males born after 1974 in the Saddleworth area (now in Greater Manchester) can still play cricket for Yorkshire. Some of the walks in this book dip into these extraneous areas.

This historical complexity is matched by the County's landscapes. Its highest points at over 2000 feet rank as mountains whilst parts of the south west are below sea level. The sharp, sudden contrasts between coastal lowlands and moorland blocs are unmatched anywhere whilst some of the secluded and sheltered upland valleys generate their own microclimates. Two of England's great rivers, the Lune and the Ribble, drain vast tracts of countryside little changed by the hand of man; relatively few roads cross or follow these waterways resulting in a legacy of unspoilt landscapes. The coastline hosts some of Britains most spectacular sand-dunes, greatest saltmarshes and sand flats; it lacks only high cliffs but the coastal limestone crags of the northwest are equally evocative.

THE BREWERIES

In common with every other county, Lancashire has seen its number of breweries decline considerably since the second war. In truth, the number in Lancashire has been decimated; there are now only four – Matthew Brown and Thwaites in Blackburn (and Matthew Brown is being closed by its parent company, Scottish and Newcastle), Moorhouses in Burnley and Mitchells in Lancaster. Even if you include the parts of Lancashire that are now in the new counties of Cumbria, Merseyside and Greater Manchester the number barely creeps into double figures, and that only if three home-brew pubs are included. Such decline has seen the demise of local favourites like Bents, Duttons, Almonds, Magees and Yates and Jackson.

Even famous regional brewers such as Chesters, Wilsons, Higsons and Oldham have succumbed to the rule of faceless accountants and profiteers. True, products bearing these names are available widely in Lancashire but they are simply names used by the marketeers of the major national breweries who took them over, asset-stripped them and then closed them down. Higsons, that most Liverpudlian of beers, is now brewed in Sheffield; Wilsons Manchester Ales in Halifax, all at the expense of taste, price and choice for the consumer. Nor has this trend subsided. In the past year nationally known names such as Greenall Whitley and Boddingtons have sold their brewing interests to concentrate on pub and leisure management; Greenalls is now brewed by Walkers, Boddingtons by Whitbread. Thankfully some regional brewers seek to remain locally based and continue to serve the interests of their local drinkers – Mitchells houses are common in the north of the County, Thwaites in the centre and Burtonwoods (brewed in north Cheshire) in the south.

Fortunately, Lancashire is well blessed with free houses and the products of well over fifty brewery companies – about a sixth of all the breweries in the country – can be sampled somewhere in the County. Thus favourites nationally such as Marstons, Theakstons and Sam Smiths can be sampled alongside more parochial beers from the likes of Joseph Holt, Hartleys and Oak Brewery. The much vaunted introduction of the right of tenants of the major brewing combines to stock and sell an additional real ale of their choice has had little impact to date in Lancashire. Many tied-house licensees appear to be biding their time and allowing themselves to gauge the success – or otherwise – of such action on pubs other than their own. One can only hope that the widely reported "difficulties" experienced by tenants of some brewery companies (e.g. not being allowed to use brewery owned glasses, bar fittings or the pub electricity supply to help purvey a guest beer) do not prevent the extension of, and success of, this long-needed change.

REAL ALE

Each of the pubs featured in this book have one thing in common, they all serve real ale on draught. In simple terms this means that the beers – milds, bitters, strong bitters, old ales and winter brews – are despatched "live" from the brewery whilst still fermenting; this secondary fermentation (so called because it supplements the primary fermentation which took place in the large brewing vessels at the brewery) continues slowly whilst the barrels are racked in the pub cellar or stillage. A spile hole allows the carbon dioxide produced by this action to escape. The matured beers are presented to the thirsty walker either direct from the barrel – a gravity drawn beer – or via a hand pump or electric pump attached to the bar. These pumping actions are the only extraneous pressure applied to the beers. Contrast this with the widely available and heavily advertised lagers and keg beers which, although brewed in exactly the same manner and from the same raw ingredients as draught, are then pasteurised (ie the fermentation is killed off) and delivered in sealed, airtight kegs to pubs. The beer is then forced out of the kegs by introducing carbon dioxide (or nitrogen oxide) under pressure into the keg; much of this gas dissolves into the liquid resulting in the gassy beers and lagers familiar to many but shunned by lovers of traditional real ales.

Looking after traditional beer is a demanding job, the landlord/cellarman working to fine tolerances of temperature and cleanliness to ensure that the beer purchased is worthy of the name real ale. The "shelf-life" of draught beer is very short and the skill needed to keep a good pint is gained only by a combination of training and experience. Real ale pubs live or die largely on the reputation of the quality (or otherwise . . .) of the beer sold; whilst a publican can do nothing to alter the quality of a bad brew from a brewery, he/she can make all the difference between a passable pint and a great one. All the licensees featured in this book strive successfully to serve a great pint – if they don't let them know; to you it's a bad pint, to them it could be the start of a slippery slope out of business.

OPENING HOURS

Under recent legislation pubs in England can now open for a maximum of twelve hours each day on Mondays to Saturdays (being 11 to 11) and for 6.5 hours on Sundays (12 to 3 and 7 to 10.30) unless extensions have been granted by local licensing magistrates. Additionally, a growing number of pubs stay open during Sunday afternoons to serve meals, with which alcohol may then be consumed on the premises

Most country pubs do not find it in their interest to take full advantage of these "relaxed" hours and tend to stick to the "traditional" hours of 12 to 3, and 6 to 11 or 7 to 11. Wherever possible I've indicated the opening hours of the pubs in this book verbatim from the mouth of the licensee; these may vary from winter to summer so, if in doubt, give the pub a ring. All the pubs open for the maximum permitted hours on Sundays.

THE WALKS

Each of the walks in this book follow rights of way to which you, as a member of the public, has unrestricted access – main and minor roads, by-ways, unadopted roads, tow-paths, bridleways and public footpaths are all part of the Queen's Highway. In addition there are concessionary and permissive footpaths, not strictly public footpaths but paths along which you have virtually unrestricted access. At the time of research and writing all routes were free from any serious restriction or blockage (except where specified) but it is the nature of the animal that public rights of way, and public footpaths in particular, are prone to short-term changes due to repair work, agricultural practices, industrial development, road and house building schemes. It is a sad reflection on the state of England and Wales's 140,000 miles of public footpaths that the results of a Countryside Commission survey carried out in 1990 suggest that your chances of completing even a modest countryside walk of only two miles without meeting access problems are a paltry one-in-three.

Definitive Rights of Way maps are prepared and maintained by staff employed by local authorities; the Ordnance Survey refer to these when updating and/or amending their series of maps. If you come across any problems on any of the walks in this book – or, indeed, on any other walk you undertake – and are certain that you are following a definitive right of way then you should initially approach the landowner to discus the problem. More often than not this will be the local farmer; they are generally pleased to talk to ramblers -who are often the first to tell them of injured animals, damaged, fences, etc. – and many maintain stiles of all descriptions to a high standard. If the problem is intractable, for example a wire fence, an impenetrable acreage of crops or a newly dug trout pond blocking the path, then you are quite within your rights to cross the fence or walk through the crops (or even swim the pond). Alternatively, in cases like this, you can try to follow the "line of least resistance" by circling a field or finding a handy farm gate; few farmers would object to you doing this although you have no legal right so to do. Unresolved problems should be reported to the Rights of Way Officer at the relevant District or Borough Council. Problems encountered whilst walking in Country Parks should be reported to the Ranger service, usually on site; on canal tow-paths to the British Waterways Board and on National Trust land to the National Trust Regional Office.

None of the walks in this book is particularly strenuous and all should be easily completed by anyone of average fitness. You'll obviously best know your own capabilities at walking but, as a rule of thumb, I'd suggest you allow a generous half an hour per mile for the walks; thus a six mile walk would take about three hours. This allows ample time for dawdling and sightseeing en route. Where particular problems do exist these are outlined in the text or highlighted at the beginning of each walk description. As for clothing, a good, comfortable, waterproof pair of boots is essential; I, personally, wouldn't countenance wellingtons as being ideal although some renowned walkers do swear by them. The rest is just common sense and largely dictatable by the weather, but do remember that, even at a height of only a few hundred feet, winds can be chilly and showers can develop virtually out of nothing, so always carry a windproof, waterproof jacket and a sweater.

The walks are grouped into generalized geographical areas, some of which are necessarily large so that all walks in one area may not be particularly contiguous. A description of each area is given in the introductory passage of the first walk in each section; the reference number of the relevant Ordnance Survey Pathfinder Series sheet(s) is given in the titles of each walk. You should have no problems in doing the walks using the sketch maps and the directions in the text, but it is always useful to have the wider perspective offered by an Ordnance Survey map to hand to help identify features of interest or to plan an alternative route should the need arise.

1. THE WEST PENNINES: ENTWISTLE

Route: Entwistle – Wayoh Reservoir – Turton Tower – Jumbles Country Park – Affetside – Hawkshaw – Edgworth

Distance: Either 11 miles or 5 miles

Map: Sheet SD 61/71 Bolton (North) and Horwich

Start: The Strawbury Duck, Entwistle

Access: The best way to get to and from this walk is by rail. Entwistle station, on the Manchester Victoria to Blackburn line, is virtually next door to the pub. Trains run hourly, Mondays to Saturdays, early morning to late evening, and two hourly on Sundays after midday. **(Timetable enquiries 061 832 8353).** If travelling by car take the A676 road from Bolton towards Burnley. About 3 miles out of Bolton at the village of Walves look for the Bulls Head on your left at a sharp corner, turn left here and drive to Edgworth. Go straight over the junction here and along Blackburn Road (nb Blackburn is signposted to the right – ignore this). Pass the red brick chapel on your left then look for the very narrow Hob Lane, also on the left (there's a signpost opposite pointing the way to Entwistle and the Strawbury Duck). Follow Hob lane to its end, crossing the reservoir en route. The pub is just over the railway bridge; parking is restricted.

The Strawbury Duck (0204 852013)

When you're doing one of the other walks in this book ask any other walker you happen upon if they've been to the Strawbury Duck. Chances are that the answer will be in the affirmative as the pub is a veritable institution amongst the walking fraternity of the North West. Slap bang in the middle of the West Pennine Moors Recreational Area and with views stretching forever, the pub is the ideal spot to relax on a summer evening after a long walk or on a winter weekend day after a shorter ramble over the frost and snow-crisped moorland.

Aside from its location the top attraction of the Strawbury Duck is the range of beers kept by landlord and proprietor Barry Speakman. The bar and side-hatch bristle with handpumps. At few places will you find a better pint of Marstons Pedigree or Tim Taylors Landlord, these being complemented by Hartleys XB, Tim Taylors Best Bitter and Golden Best and an endless variety of guest beers (Pendle Witches Brew being a favourite). If you're there in the depths of winter you'll also usually find a barrel of monumentally strong winter ale on stillage behind the bar and a powerful home-concocted mulled wine. The Duck is also widely renowned for its range of bar food including a great range of Indian dishes.

The pub was originally called The Station Hotel (no prizes....) and owned by the now-defunct Duttons brewery. Twice they tried to close the pub, in 1965 and 1970, but each time the axe failed to fall. After the second time it became a free house and acquired the unusual name. It had long been known to locals as the Strawberry due to the colour of the stonework in the setting sun. The owner of the new free house freely adapted this name, changing the berry to bury after the town a few miles away and adding duck as a variation of his own surname, Duxbury, hence Strawbury Duck. The name stuck and this idiosyncratic whim became part of ramblers folklore.

A warren of small rooms and nooks radiate from the bar area, generally stone slabbed with beamed ceilings and warmed by open log fires. Half of the pub is the old Station Hotel, about a century old, the other half was added in 1981 with the addition of the adjoining 300 year old cottage. It is very much of a family pub at weekends when it is open all day (Saturday noon – 11pm, Sunday noon – 10.30 pm, with a supper licence so you can drink with your meal during the afternoon). For the rest of the week the hours are noon – 3 pm and 7 pm – 11 pm but it's closed on Monday lunchtimes (except Bank Holidays). Food orders end half an hour before closing time.

THE WEST PENNINE MOORS

Rambling along on either of the two walks in this piece you're right in the heart of The West Pennine Moors, a distinct bloc of the Pennine chain bounded to the north by the River Darwen and to the south by the "mill towns" of Bolton and Bury. The area is characterised by high moorland tracts – some of the highest land in Lancashire – deep wooded cloughs, eerie remains of long abandoned quarries and a plethora of lakes. These latter features are all artificial, the more than generous rainfall of the area stored up to slake the thirst of Liverpudlians, Boltonians and Buryites. The largest and most spectacular are those in the far west at Anglezarke and Rivington, nearly 150 years old; the most

The Strawbury Duck

picturesque are those visited on this walk in the twin valleys of the Bradshaw and Broadhead Brooks.

Prior to flooding these same valleys saw the birth of the industrial revolution, farmers doubling as weavers using local wool, the power of the streams to drive simple machinery and the water to wash, shrink and bleach the product. Production of fustian, a mix of cotton fibres and linen, was also important by the 1600's, only in the nineteenth century did the familiar cotton towns develop from this Tudor base. Many of the dour, mullioned gritstone manor houses that still dot the area – Entwistle Old Hall for example – and the small "Folds" of cottages came about thanks to the wealth generated from this embryonic industrial revolution.

THE WALK

Two walks are suggested in this area, both have a common first two miles and final mile. From the pub cross the railway bridge and follow the road downhill. Having passed the breeze block stables on your left

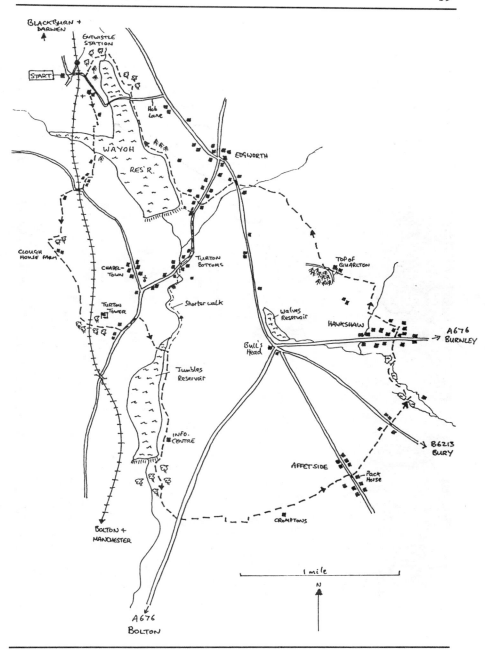

turn right up the track opposite a lamppost and walk up between a barn and Entwistle Old Hall. Just past the barn look for a stile on the left, cross it and walk ahead across the small pasture to the stone slab stile, passing through this and walking across the field ahead, reaching the far side about 30 yards up from the row of cottages. Wind through the gaps in the barbed wire, looking to your right for a short walled path leading up to a stile. Climb this stile (by a waymark signpost) and turn left to a further stile. Once over this descend the steps and follow the path as it winds right, sinking deeply between high, tree lined banks. At the end the path issues onto a causeway across an arm of Wayoh Reservoir. To your right the Bolton-Blackburn railway crosses the drowned Armsgrove

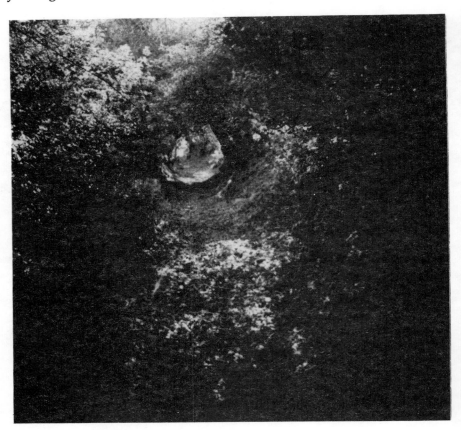

Sunken Trackway, Entwistle

Clough on its sombre viaduct, to your left drink in the extensive views over to Holcombe Moor and Harcles Hill. Wildfowl on the reservoir include Great Crested Grebe, a multitude of species of duck and the ubiquitous heron and kingfisher.

At the end of the causeway leave the main path and go straight ahead up the narrow path with the tiny clough to your immediate right. Pass through the stile at the top and walk along the partly paved path to reach the drive to Armsgrove Farm. Continue ahead along this and at the end turn right to enter the tiny fold of cottages. Walk along past these solid old cottages and the parsonage, bear right along past the cupressor hedge and walk to Greens Arms Road. Here turn right and cross the railway bridge, then walk straight ahead along the drive to Lowes Moor. Stick with the drive as it passes to the right of the small Georgian mansion, curve round behind the redeveloped barn and go through the tall gate to the left of the farm gate. Cross the brook, then the stile to the right of the next gate and walk up to the right along the field edge. From the next stile sight the line of trees ahead – the ones with the buildings peeking through – and cross the rough pasture to these, fording a narrow clough en route. On reaching the wall this side of the trees turn right and walk up to the surfaced moorland road, turning left along this and cross the cattle grid.

Pass by Clough House Farm, where there are some peculiar octagonal brick towers, and follow the track along keeping the wall to your immediate left and ignoring any tracks off to the right. The rounded moorland top on your right is Cheetham Close on top of which are the scant remains of a stone circle. Pass through the gate stile at the end of the track and fall away left along the track down the wooded clough. At the end of this you should cross the railway on the castellated folly bridge, built to mirror nearby Turton Tower for the owner at the time, James Kay, a noted local industrialist and director of the railway company. Continuing downhill, the Tower comes into view on your left. It is said to be a Pele Tower (more common in Northumberland and the northern Lakes) with Elizabethan "magpie" additions. Inside is an Alladin's cave of armour, medieval weaponry and Tudor furniture and a remarkable chandelier made from stag's antlers. The Hall belongs to Blackburn Council and is open to the public (phone 0204 852203 for details).

Walk down to the main road and turn left, then at the bottom of the slope take the signposted path off to the right which leads past the pill-box. Pass by the pond at the crest of the hill and enter the woodland beyond, following the path through the trees to emerge at a bridge across the top end of Jumbles Reservoir. Cross this bridge. It is at this point that the shorter and longer walks diverge.

Turton Tower

Shorter Walk

Once across this bridge turn left and walk along the path beside the reservoir which soon peters out to become the feeder brook, Bradshaw Brook. Simply remain with the path and pass the terrace of three storey houses to reach a factory car park. Bear left across the bridge out of the car park and walk up to the main road in this, the hamlet of Turton Bottoms. When you reach the road turn right and walk steeply uphill to reach the Black Bull pub, from beside which a footpath leads to the eastern bank of Wayoh Reservoir. Walk up along this path which here rejoins the route of the longer walk (now go to the final paragraph).

Longer Walk

Turn right off the bridge and walk along the path which skirts the reservoir. Much of this bank is a nature reserve, so observe the restriction notices. After a while the path climbs away from the reservoir and reaches the Information Centre for Jumbles Country Park (open Easter to October on Wednesday, Saturday, Sunday and Bank Holiday afternoons and on Sunday afternoons only during the winter). Beyond this is the Warden's office and large car park. Aim for the far right hand corner of this car park and walk down the steps, turning right at the bottom. In a matter of twenty or so yards bear left and follow the path up the hillside through the oak woodlands, an old mill leat gradually falling away to your right. Cross the stile beside the gate and walk up along the track to the main road.

Go straight across this road and up along the surfaced track leading to Cromptons Farm. Skirt around to the right of the covered reservoir and walk on uphill until the farmhouse is just off to your right. Your way now lies straight ahead; the track, however, has been infilled with rubble. A path through this is taking shape so do your best to follow it – aim to walk up along the line of pylons. There are good views from this point, Darwen's Jubilee Tower and Bolton's Town Hall are easily discernible landmarks. Where the infill ends just carry straight on up the field, cross the stile at the end and walk up to the road at the hamlet of Affetside. This is the line of the Roman road between Manchester and Ribchester. Turning right brings you almost immediately to The Pack Horse Inn, another favourite haunt of local ramblers and rambling clubs and offering handpumped Hydes Anvil Ales.

Thirst quenched, take the path that goes to the left of the pub and alongside the car park; it soon becomes a walled pathway leading down off the ridge. Directly ahead is the second of Lancashire's famous three towers, Peel's monument, high above Ramsbottom. The extensive views from here also include the flat – topped Knowle Hill, Saddleworth Moor and the Dark Peak. Remain with this path, pass by the house to your left and walk to the minor road. Here turn right and walk to the telephone box just beyond the cottages. Turn left here at the footpath sign, cross the stile at the end of the garden and walk down the field with the hedge to your right.

Beneath the dead tree cross the stile and walk across the dam between the two mill lodges. Bear right at the far end of this dam and walk down a few stone steps to the thorn bush, turning left at this point and gradually descending the hillside, walking in the general direction of a white painted house on the hillside ahead. Stick with the path, passing below a chimney stack and above the remains of a mill. At one point you have to ford a narrow stream, approached beneath a fallen tree. Up to the left here is a waterfall, well hidden in a wooded cleft in the hillside. Continue to contour-walk past a further mill lodge and then work gradually right to the gate in the corner of the field near the old caravan. Cross the stile here and turn right along the track across the dam of a further, landscaped, lodge.

At the crossing of tracks by the Hawkshaw Tennis Club sign turn left and walk up to the single main street of Hawkshaw, crossing straight over and walking up Hawkshaw Lane. In about 200 yards you reach Tonge Fold Cottage on your right. On your left at this point a public footpath sign points the way along a driveway. Go along here for about 40 yards and angle left along the narrow path just before the garage – there's a home made footpath sign pointing the way. Pass through the stile at the end and walk ahead down across the pasture to the drive. Cross the stile here and then turn right and walk across the bridge, remaining with the gently rising track for several hundred yards. At the point where the lone wooden post stands to your right look up left to sight the line of an old wall up the hillside (if you've reached the lone thorn bush you've gone too far) and walk up the line of this wall to the stile at the crest. Cross this and walk uphill to the barn adjoining Top of Quarlton Farm.

Go across the stile to the left of the gate on the left of the barn and walk to the farm drive. Look half left here to find a waymark arrow directing you up the outside of the farmhouse's garden. Walk up beside this wall and then several yards of wooden rail fencing to a wide stile immediately before the metal gate on your right and at a bend in the track; there's a plantation of fir trees on your left. Cross this, walk ahead to the cross fence and turn left to the stile in the corner. Cross this and walk to the corner of the wire fence, then bear half right and walk down across the field to a further stile near an old oil drum, a few yards from the field corner. Once over this follow the path ahead, remaining some way above the floor of the shallow valley down to your right. Keep your eyes on the fence in the valley, however, and when you see the waymark arrow cross this fence and walk to the left along the embankment. You'll have to leave this to go through the wire fence that cuts this embankment (gate to your left) but regain it and walk to its end.

Cross the rough track and walk ahead across the pasture, looking for a frame stile at the far side just beyond the row of thorn trees. Once over this head down across the next field aiming for the corner of the wall pointing directly at you. At this corner is a stone slab stile through which you should pass, then following the line of the fence on your right down to the stream. Turn downstream and look for the stile on the far bank, reaching this via the large boulders in the stream. Once over the stile climb up to the path and turn left to reach the minor road at a gateway some yards above a garage.

Turn right up the road towards Edgworth village, but before reaching such enter the field on the left at the footpath sign immediately before the cottages. Walk virtually straight ahead up the short climb (aim for the nearest pylon) to the wall surrounding the junior school playing field. Keep this immediately on your right and walk around the playing fields, then along the muddy walled track. On reaching the modern houses walk along the narrow path on your side of them to the narrow track which leads you up, right, past the old cottages (dated 1756) on Park Lane to the main road. Cross this and turn left, then about 50 yards along turn up along Harbour Lane, just past the bungalows. Walk along to the end of Harbour Lane and cross the small stile which is marked with a hydrant sign and is immediately to the right of the drive of the last house on the left. Walk on to a further stile a matter of yards away, cross this and walk ahead to the path alongside Wayoh Reservoir, turning right along this. The name "Wayoh" is derived from the Old English words for "path along a ridge."

From this point (where the shorter walk rejoins) remain with the path up along this eastern bank of the reservoir. Cross over the narrow road (Hob Lane) and continue on through the trees, the reservoir gradually becoming reedy and silted off to your left. When you reach the green-based footbridge over Broadhead Brook cross it and walk along the track ahead, shortly coming to another footbridge which you should also cross. From here walk straight ahead and take the left hand path of the two that go up the hillside in front of you (ie the one without the stile). Follow this path up through the trees to a stile, cross this and then climb the steep pasture to another stile. Go over this and walk uphill along the road back to the pub.

2. THE WEST PENNINES: HELMSHORE

Route: Helmshore – Grane Valley – Haslingden Grane – Windy Harbour

Distance: 6.5 Miles

Map: Sheet SD 62/72 Blackburn

Start: The Robin Hood, Helmshore

Access: Helmshore is one mile south of Haslingden on the B6214 road to Bury. The Robin Hood is on the B6235 Holcombe Road, about 150 yards north of the Helmshore Textile Museums; the easiest thing is to follow the brown road signs to the Museums which are well signposted locally and from the main A56 dual carriageway.

The Robin Hood (0706 213180)

Remember Adam Adamant? The be-swordsticked Victorian detective frozen in a block of ice by fiendish Chinese villains only to be thawed out in 1960's London. If he'd thawed out in The Robin Hood in 1991 he'd feel immediately at home as the pub has been as if in amber since it first became a licensed premises in the 1880's. True, he'd find the various electric games machines an anachronism but, these apart, it's as unspoilt a pub as you'll find anywhere.

It would be easy to overlook the tiny roadside pub nestling in the narrow gorge of the Ogden Brook, one blink and you'd have passed it by. The small bar serves three interconnecting rooms hollowed out of this ground floor of the two mill-workers cottages it once was. Open fires warm tiny rooms decorated with watercolours, brasses, prints, mill shuttles, an old cornet and – as you can't fail to notice – ducks. Landlord Colin Ruleman obviously has a thing about our aquatic feathered friends; there are brass ducks and porcelain ducks, pot ducks and wicker ducks, flying ducks and prints of ducks. Even the ends of the seat in front of the pub are duck shaped. And if you look out of the windows at the side or back you'll see the real thing on the Ogden Brook or one of the mill ponds that the pub overlooks. The nearest pond has been stocked with goldfish and Koi carp which may be immune to ducks but not to the heron or kingfishers which you can watch from the windows or from the tiny beer garden that hangs precariously high over the water.

These ponds and the river, together with the steep, tree-lined slope beyond, give the pub an enviable position in this old established industrial area; Higher Mill and Whittaker's Mill (which the ponds serve) look nothing less than picturesque, a rare accolade for such "Dark Satanic" buildings. To help you enjoy the setting is an excellently kept pint of handpumped Tetley's Mild or Bitter – ignore the Wilson's sign outside, it's just another anachronism. The pub also keeps spirits. Or at least one, the ghost of an old mill worker christened Wilf. As many as forty people used to live in the cottages before the pub was developed and Wilf is finding it impossible to leave. Perhaps he likes the beer (Colin Ruleman has had pint pots mysteriously move about the pub overnight) or the regular live music sessions, usually folk, jazz or cajun). Even an exorcism in the 1980's failed to persuade the ghost to leave, Colin's dog certainly still senses a presence from time to time although Colin himself has yet to achieve a sighting.

The Robin Hood is open between 4 pm and 11 pm on Mondays to Wednesdays and from noon to 11 pm on Thursdays to Saturdays. There's no food but, as a recent newspaper feature on the pub suggests, you could always take your own crumpet to toast over the Victorian grates.

Helmshore Textile Museums

Two adjoining but unconnected old mills are now the focal point of this, the major working museum of Lancashire's textile and weaving heritage. Higher Mill, the older of the two mills and built in 1789, is a woollen fulling mill complete with fully operational fulling stocks powered by a water wheel. The wheel is fed from the long, narrow mill pond above the mill in the deep winding gorge of the Ogden Brook. Fulling was the process by which loosely woven fabrics were converted into tightly knitted cloth, the broadcloth which was the staple material on which the whole of the vast woollen textile industry of Lancashire was based. The initial loose fabric was soaked in water, impregnated with Fullers Earth to disperse unwanted natural oils and then hammered flat on the fulling stocks. The mill last worked commercially in 1967 and much restoration work, including a rebuilding of the water wheel in 1978, has produced a fine live museum. Higher Mill also houses the leading collection of early carding and spinning machines including a spinning jenny and an Arkwrights water frame.

The adjoining Whittakers Mill is a Victorian cotton spinning mill which used a steam powered condenser system to convert cotton waste into material such as flannelette, its last productive year was 1978. This is the major part of the museum housing a comprehensive history of the Lancashire wool, cotton and flax industries, with working spinning mules and carding engines taking up virtually the whole of one floor. Opening hours vary through the year, for details telephone 0706 226459.

The Grane Valley

It's hard to believe but only a century ago this quiet, virtually deserted valley was a hive of activity with weaving, quarrying, farming and even illegal whisky distilling keeping well over 1000 folk occupied in a thriving upland community. The rise of the factory system put paid to the weaving, economics saw off most of the farming families and all but two of the quarries. Whatever happened to the illegal stills? The thirst for water to satisfy the burgeoning population and industries of Bury, nine miles to the south, also played its part with a string of reservoirs being created between 1850 and 1912 drowning productive pastureland. Probably only a couple of dozen people now live in the valley which is littered with the gaunt ruins of old farmhouses and cottages, the eerie wastes of long abandoned and overgrown quarries and criss crossed by half forgotten moorland roads, tracks and paths. The Information Centre at Clough Head Quarry, just off the route of the walk, is the place to visit to gain greater insight into this fascinating, little known corner of Lancashire. It is open between Easter and October on Wednesday, Saturday, Sunday and Bank Holiday afternoons.

The Walk

Go uphill from the Robin Hood, the river and sinuous mill pond down to your right, overshadowed by the viaduct of the long dead railway. Pass a small terrace of cottages on your right and a second terrace on your left. Immediately past this second terrace a public footpath sign directs you up the track behind the houses towards Musbury Heights. Walk up this, bear right at the fork and cross the stile by the gate. Continue uphill, bear right at the top to pass between a barn and a ruined house, walking on to the end of the track. The distinctive "Table Mountain" hill on the left is Tor Hill. Cross the stile at the end and turn right up the rutted track, shortly passing by the ivy covered gable of the

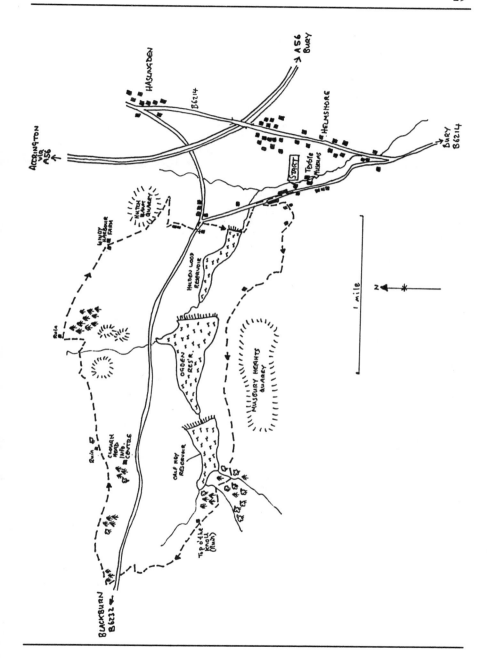

old farm on your right. Go straight ahead up the hedged track, crossing two stiles, over the bank at the end and straight ahead up the field road. Pass through the gate at the end, walk up to the fork and bear right, following the rough track around the snout of the hill.

Walk round the corner, the views opening out eastwards over Holden Wood Reservoir, ignoring the first turn right. At the second turn, no more than a large gap in the wall and bank, bear right and look for the stile just to the right of the two small thorn bushes below you. Cross this and look for the ladder stile down to your left. Just follow the line of the stream down, walk behind the rebuilt house and cross the stile, then the ladder stile. Turn left and follow the line of broken wall and fence along the hillside, working your way gradually downhill to reach the new wooden gate and rail fencing, beside which is a stile to cross. From here walk ahead along the well maintained footpath, passing by the foot of an old incline which once carried waggons bearing gritstone blocks and flagstones down from the huge quarries on Musbury Heights, far up to your left.

With Ogden Reservoir to your right wind along with the path, gradually working uphill to pass round the top of a deeply incised clough. Bear right here, ignoring the concessionary path off to the left (which leads up to the old quarry workings, a worthwhile detour if you have time) and contour walk along the path for a further half mile or so. Pass by the isolated tree, above the dam of Calf Hey Reservoir, and continue on for about 100 yards, then follow the waymark arrow along the lower path. This is part of the Rossendale Way, a waymarked route which offers a long circuit of the Borough of Rossendale.

Just before the woodland cross the slatted wooden footbridge and climb the steps, zig-zagging round and over the two stiles to join the path across the top of the woods. Cross a further board footbridge, climb the steps and then turn left along the path at the top. Follow this along and over a further footbridge hidden in a deep clough, then walk along for about 60 yards to the point where the path bends left and passes a final tree on the right. Just beyond this point, and before you reach the old stone gateposts, a waymark post off to your left marks your route. Simply follow the waymarks up the hillside to end up at the top corner of the plantation of conifers. From here continue as indicated by the waymarkers, crossing stiles as necessary to end up at the substantial ruins of Top o' th' Knoll Farm. Work your way round the left hand side of these and follow the track across the hillside beyond.

Remain with this old, walled, in places paved track, passing several more ruins to reach a small waterfall down to your right. Beyond this the route of the track is barred by a wall between two gateposts. Cross the stream and track at this point and then continue to follow its line, keeping it just to your left until past the boggy section. Walk along for about 400 yards and then bear right with the hairpin. A few yards on follow the direction of the waymark to the left, walk up across the field and climb the stile to gain the main road – just head for the left hand corner of the small plantation on the hillside. Cross straight over the road and follow the rough track and stream up beside the trees. At the top climb the rickety stile and turn right.

For the next two miles the route of the walk is alongside the wall to your right, crossing stiles as necessary. In a mile or so you'll see Clough Head Quarry car park and Information Centre down to your right; should you wish to visit this then the path to it is waymarked from a point immediately before the isolated group of trees you reach. Pass the trees and a working quarry soon becomes visible off to the right. You should remain well up from this, following the occasional yellow waymark arrow. In a short while walk downhill to pass along the embankment above an abandoned quarry site. Cross the stream and climb the steep clough side, aiming for the ruins by the lone tree, near to which is a waymarker directing you straight ahead.

After a short distance go through the gap in the wall by the waymark arrow and aim for the bottom right hand corner of the field, from where a further waymarker on a post directs you to some trees by a ruin. Walk to the moorland road here and turn left, walking uphill for about 150 yards to the tree beside the gate on your right. Climb the stile here and walk along the track through the old gateposts, following the wall on your right. Keep to the left of the tall wall you come to and go through the gate, following the track along until you reach Windy Harbour Farm. Pass the first barn and then turn right, go through the yard gate and walk along the track past a further barn and away from the farm. At the end of this track go through the gate ahead and follow the track around the lip of the quarry.

This large quarry, Hutch Bank, is still working, but you see little despite its proximity. What you do get is enormous views in virtually every direction. Walk gradually downhill with the track to the point where the fence falls away to the right and the road curves away to the left. Fall along with the fence to reach a very precarious stile on your right. Cross this and walk along the old track, climb over a gate and continue downhill. At the bottom the track meets another at a very sharp angle. Turn sharp left here and then in a matter of yards climb the bank on your right to the corner of a wall. From here sight the white painted cottage below you and walk to it, go down the track beside it, pass through the gap stile at the end and walk on down to the main road.

Cross the road and turn left, passing by the church to reach the hamlet of Holden Wood. Turn right down the road towards Helmshore and then immediately past the Holden Arms pub car park turn right along the narrow road to Holden Wood Reservoir. Cross the dam and bear right. Immediately on your left take the path up behind the retaining wall and follow the line of fence on your right. As this ends walk ahead along the path which descends through an area of scrubby woodland to the road at the bottom. Turn right along this to return to the Robin Hood.

Higher Mill (left) and Whittaker's Mill, Helmshore

3. THE WEST PENNINES: BELMONT

Route: Belmont – Longworth Clough – Dimple – Longworth Moor

Distance: 7 Miles

Map: Sheet SD 61/71 Bolton (North) and Horwich

Start: The Black Dog, Belmont, Bolton

Access: Belmont village is some 5 miles north of Bolton on the A675 road to Preston. The Black Dog is on the left about 200 yards after the sharp bend that heralds the village. The entrance to the car park is off the minor road signposted to Rivington, the pub itself is on the corner of this road and the A675.

The Black Dog (020481 218)

This is the northernmost pub in the tied estate of the small Manchester family brewery of Joseph Holt; in all there are only about a hundred pubs. These choice beers, which have a fanatical following, are nationally renowned as being the cheapest in Britain. The bitter is dark and very bitter, the mild very dark and slightly fruity; both are kept particularly well in this moorland edge pub.

The Black Dog was built as a farmhouse in the 1750's. In 1825 the middle part of the farm was converted into a pub and it remained a farm-cum-pub until the 1930's, beer was brewed on site until the late 'Twenties. In 1952 Holts purchased the pub from the local butcher. During the Nineteenth century the village court was held in what is now the snug, directly opposite the bar. The jurors benches remain set into the walls of this tiny area, the local squire, also the magistrate for the area, sat at the end of the bench distinguished by an additional arm rest.

The pub has a connection with a famous local murder. In 1838 a Scottish pedlar named George Henderson, who lived locally, had made his regular walk across nearby Winter Hill from the Horwich side to the Black Dog. En route back to Horwich he was waylaid and murdered high on the lonely moors; the site on Winter Hill is marked by a plaque and simple monument known as Scotchman's Stump.

Every available beam in the pub is festooned with old pewter tankards and pint pots, steins and toby jugs; there's even a potty (possibly a variation on a yard of ale?). The walls are crammed full of framed prints and old photographs and every nook and cranny (of which there are legion) houses an oddment or artefact. If all this sounds rather kitsch, it is not – the building was seemingly built specifically to house such ornamentation.

Landlord Jim Pilkington has amassed an enormous collection of classical music tapes which provide background music throughout the day, often drowned out by the idle chatter of both locals and ramblers who ensure the pub always has a lively atmosphere or by Jim himself who's an accomplished whistler (Roger Whittaker eat your heart out). The pub has a large function room which is regularly used by such as the local hang gliding club (Winter Hill is renowned as a hang gliding location despite the television mast) and the pot holing and caving club. The classical music theme is occasionally picked up in all-but impromptu concerts given by a ten piece (or more) orchestra made up of members of the Hallé, the Northern Chamber Orchestra and other internationally known musicians – all for fun and to benefit local charities.

The Black Dog is open from noon to 4 pm (3 pm on Tuesday and Wednesday) and from 7 pm to 11 pm. Bar meals are available daily from noon to 2 pm and 7 pm to 9 pm (8.30 pm on Sundays, no evening meals on Mondays or Tuesdays). Children and dogs are welcome, and if you want to discover the West Pennines in depth then you can stay at the pub, the old stables have recently been converted into three letting rooms.

Belmont

This is a small moorland village about 850 feet above sea level straggling up the northern bank of the Horden Brook. The original hamlet was called Horden but was renamed in about 1800 by the owner and developer of the calico and print works which gave rise to much of the housing in the village. Maria Square, opposite the pub car park, was built first in 1804, soon followed by piecemeal developments of tiny squares and terraces, some of the latter built on a hillside so steep that they have two storeys at the front but four at the rear. The calico works closed in the 1860's but a dye and bleach works opened soon afterwards and this remains in operation today, though the possibility of its closure and replacement by "executive" housing is the subject of a current planning application. The village is dominated by the brooding mass of

Winter Hill, at around 1500 feet the highest point in the West Pennines area and itself capped by a giant television transmitter mast.

Black Dog, Belmont

The Walk

From the pub car park cross the main road and walk down the street known as Maria Square. The green to the right will often be bustling with dozens of duck which alternatively use the old lodges visible to the left at the bottom end of the Square. At the foot of the hill carry straight on along the road through the dyeing and bleaching works and uphill beyond. Shortly after you've passed the two cottages on your right is a walled enclosure and parking spot also on the right. Immediately before this is a stone step stile into the pasture. Walk down this pasture, cross the stile at the bottom and walk across the long wooden footbridge, closely followed by the dam which holds back an "Ornamental Reservoir."

Turn left at the end of the dam and follow the course of the mill leat on your right, remaining with this for the best part of a mile. A little way along a series of waterfalls lie well hidden down to the left in the deep wooded clough of Horden Brook. In the summer months the path is lined with a veritable forest of Himalayan Balsam and the leat is a popular fishing ground with heron and kingfisher.

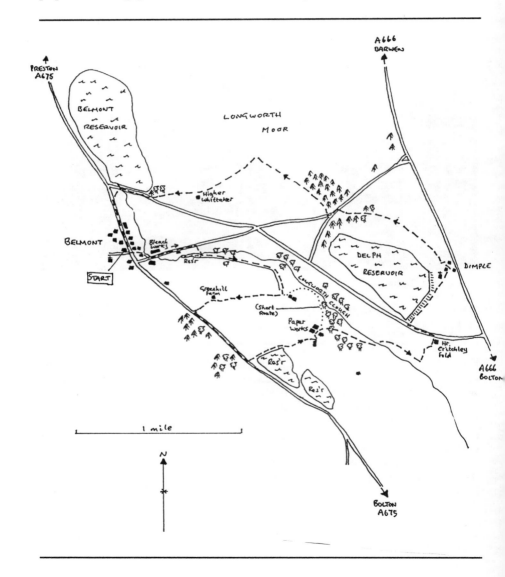

Walk around the hillside with the leat and then a few yards beyond to reach the farm road. At the time of writing (November 1990) the right of way further along Horden Brook, which here is the Longworth Clough Nature Reserve, is blocked by massive excavation works being undertaken at the paper mill in the valley, so a diversionary route is outlined below. It is to be hoped that the route through the Nature Reserve to the mill will be reinstated once the work is complete. If/when it is your route would now be left and then left again just before the barn. Work down to the valley floor and follow the brook downstream, then walk up the side of the woods to the far bottom end of the factory buildings. From here the path is obvious, leading down away from the factory and into the woodlands. Locally, walkers have been forging an unofficial alternative route below the workings and mill to regain the right of way some way downstream.

The diversionary route means that you turn right along the farm track and follow it to the main road about half a mile distant, turning left at Greenhill Farm to reach the road. Turn left along the road and walk for a further half mile to a gated entrance, on your left, into North West Water property, there's a field gate and the footpath gate is next to this. Walk along the embankment of Springs Reservoir and then stick straight ahead with the track as the embankment curves away to the right. Follow this track across the pasture to emerge on a rough road just below the terrace of cottages. Turn left and, at the bottom, follow the roadway down into the mill complex (yes, it is a public footpath). Wind with the road through the complex and at the bottom end walk ahead into the woodlands, the point where the shorter, blocked route is rejoined.

Walk down through the woods and then alongside the stream, crossing this via the wooden footbridge several hundred yards downstream. Once on the opposite bank bear right and follow the wide path down along the field. Where this path splits at a stone bridge bear left (don't cross the bridge) and then very shortly left again at the end of the fence, scrambling up the slope to the stile. Cross this and follow the fence on your left up to the next stile, from here aiming for the left of Higher Critchley Fold Farm. Pass through the gap stile in the wall, turn left and left again along the minor road. Follow this for several hundred yards to the grassy face of Delph Reservoir's dam, whereupon turn right along the path at the foot of this slope.

The path leads across a massive stone footbridge over the outflow stream from the reservoir and up a walled track to the hamlet of Dimple.

At the end of this track you reach a small chapel and school on your left. The chapel is Walmersley Unitarian Chapel and dates from 1713. The inside is a delight with wooden box pews and a large wooden balcony around three walls; if it is locked you can see well enough through the windows. The adjoining school dates from 1851.

Walk up beside the graveyard and then bear left at the end along the cobbled road past the houses. This soon deteriorates into a rough track; at the point where it hairpins to the right you should turn left and cross the stile by the green gate. Skirt the wood and bear right at the fork, following the track across the moorland. Enter the wood ahead and, some way on, bear right at the low footpath signpost, almost immediately crossing the head of a small waterfall. Walk on through the woods, leaving them by a stile and walk across the pasture. At the far end carefully cross the decrepit footbridge and walk up to the minor road.

Join this road and turn left, remaining with it to the end of the woods and there turning right, following the track you join up past the woods and out onto the open moor. Stick to the track, crossing through gates as necessary, until you reach the old, lonely signpost, its legend too weather-beaten to read. It points to the right, you want to turn left and follow the obvious path across the boggy moor, heading directly for the Winter Hill transmitter. From here there is an extensive view to the left across the Greater Manchester basin to the Peak District beyond. Cross a stile and aim for the small enclosure of newly planted trees; keep these on your left and follow the line of the wall on your right. Cross the sunken driveway behind Higher Whittaker Farm and then head half left across the field, aiming for the corner of the copse near which a stile gives access to a minor road. Turn right along this road and walk along over the dam of Belmont Reservoir. At the far end follow the path up to the left, join the main road and walk down into the village of Belmont to reach the Black Dog about 500 yards away.

4. THE WEST PENNINES: WHEELTON

Route: Wheelton – Leeds & Liverpool Canal – Withnell Fold – Brinscall – Wheelton Plantation

Distance: 7 miles

Map: Sheet SD 62/72 Blackburn

Start: The Dressers Arms, Wheelton

Access: The village of Wheelton is off the A674 Chorley to Blackburn road about three miles north-east of Chorley and two miles north-east of Junction 8 on the M61. To reach The Dressers Arms, which is at the east end of the village, drive past the Red Cat pub/restaurant and remain on the A674 as it bypasses the village to the south, then take the minor road which branches to the right and is signposted to Brinscall. The Dressers is on your left just a few yards up along this road.

The Dressers Arms (0254 830041)

There's been a pub here since well before the time of Oliver Cromwell. The "Inn on Friars Brow" was named to reflect the Brothers of a Friary which once stood at the top of the lane, since corrupted to "Briars Brow." Cromwell's persecution of Catholics in the area included these Brothers, nothing now remains of their former home. The pub's current name celebrates the craft of the stone dresser, the skilled workers who once laboured in the now-defunct quarry a few hundred yards from the pub. Old photographs of these craftsmen are a strong feature of the decor of the pub, its low beamed ceilings complementing the solid stone structure and massive fireplaces.

Until the late 1950's the pub was the smallest in Lancashire, just a small stillage, serving hatch and drinking room. Extensions into neighbouring cottages, once the homes of the quarry foremen, saw this claim to fame extinguished, the "new" pub now having a separate games room, lounge and snug all within easy reach of the popular bar. Reasons for this popularity include Marstons Pedigree, Boddingtons Bitter and their own-label Dressers Bitter and Mild as well as a variety of guest beers. Also on offer is an extensive range of bar snacks including such delights as Mussels Hotpot, Spicey Stuffed Peppers and Seafood Pie, all at a price which makes them a contender for the title of Lancashire's champion pub food bargain. For those who feel the need to crown a walk with a full-blown meal an a-la-carte and seafood restaurant fills the first floor rooms above the pub.

Dressers Arms, Wheelton

Landlord Phil Smithies welcomes children and often hosts groups of ramblers; in the wettest of weather please wear boot protectors (e.g. plastic bags) or leave your boots in the porch. Opening hours are 11 am to 3 pm, and 5.30 pm to 11 pm; bar meals are available from noon to 2 pm and 7 pm to 10 pm.

Withnell Fold

This hamlet owes its existence entirely to the Parke family who made a fortune from the cotton industry in nearby Preston. Diversifying from this industry, in 1843 the Parkes' opened a paper mill on the bank of the canal at Withnell Fold Farm. To house the workers a "model" village was built, the benevolent Parkes' also provided a reading room, shop, chapel and other communal facilities. The village survives intact although the mill, latterly used to produce banknote paper, closed nearly 25 years ago; part of it was demolished and part taken over by small engineering and electrical firms which still thrive there. In recent years new housing has been added to the old core of the village and "executive" homes, many converted from old mill outbuildings and the reading room, overlook the canal. The village stocks remain in place on one side of the village square, a few yards away the old village farm is still in business and a nature reserve is planned to enhance this already idyllic spot.

Leeds & Liverpool Canal

One of England's major waterways, this cross-Pennine route took 43 years to complete from its inception in 1773 to the final link in 1817, delays being due both to financial problems and the Napoleonic wars. Some of the greatest feats of canal engineering help take the canal between the two great northern cities which it links – the mile long Burnley Embankment, the Bingley five-rise locks and the near-mile long Foulridge tunnel for example. The stretch of canal followed on this walk is perhaps the most scenic along its 127 mile length, contouring the hillside high above a meandering stream, well wooded and with distant views of the Pennine hills. It is very busy during the summer months with pleasure craft, less so in winter when it is rich with wildlife.

The Walk

From the Dressers walk down to the main road and cross straight over, heading down Victoria Street. A short distance downhill take the footpath signposted to the right up Stable Lane and walk up to the end. As you get to the house at the top look to your right to find the gate into the field, turn left and walk up this field. At the far end leave by the stile next to the gate and walk straight ahead up the rutted track. Enter the field at the end and stick to the left hand boundary, working left and downhill through the copse of chestnut trees to the lane at the foot of the slope. The view from this stand of trees extends over the nearby canal and across the Lancashire Plain cut by low, wooded ridges; on the horizon the large gasometer is a (in)famous landmark at the coastal resort of Southport.

Turn right along the lane and then, immediately before reaching the red brick bungalow, turn left down along the track, cross the canal bridge and turn left, following the canal north with the water on your right. A great variety of birds may be encountered in the next mile or so on the

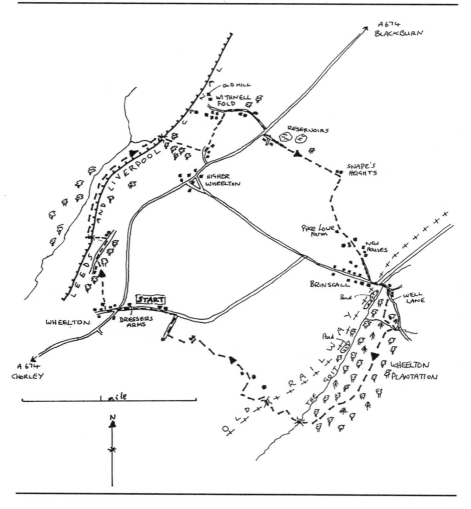

canal or down in the valley on the left. Watch out for kingfisher, coot, moorhen, little owl, sparrowhawk, kestrel, herons and jays to name but a few. You can see where the canal trough has recently undergone major repairs, a new concrete tow-path on the near bank and tons of small limestone blocks on the far side to help prevent the wash created by boats eroding the steep wooded slope above.

Follow the tow-path for about a mile. On your left a rusting mileage post records the distances to the terminal points of the canal whilst ahead the tall brick chimney at Withnell Fold peeks above the trees. Just before Bridge 87 – the number is bolted to the bridge above the water – leave the tow-path via the stile on the left, walk up to and cross the bridge and bear half right along the path at the far end. Follow the path along the side of the valley, gradually rising up to the crest before reaching the massive aqueduct on your right. This is part of the complex system of pipelines developed to carry water from Thirlmere and other lakes in the Lake District to, initially, Manchester and more recently to other towns in mid and south Lancashire. Carry on along the crest of the valley aiming for the group of cottages in the middle distance, pausing for a moment to take in the view to the left which includes the fortified Hoghton Tower on the distant wooded hillcrest, with the bulk of Longridge Fell forming the horizon.

The field narrows to a track before reaching the cottages. Cross the stile and bear left this side of the cottages, following the rough track through the gate and across a field to reach the hamlet of Withnell Fold. Follow the track straight ahead until reaching the cobbled road. The route here is to the right but it's worth diverting left to walk down to the square and, beyond this, the old mill and the canal in this, one of the first planned industrial villages.

Walk up to the main road and cross straight over, walking a short way up Oakmere Avenue and then up the left fork. The road gradually deteriorates into a rough track passing housing to your right and two reservoirs on your left. Carry straight ahead up the track which eventually fetches up at an isolated farm, Snape's Heights, near the hilltop. Walk ahead through the yard, cross the stile to the right of the gate and turn right, heading for the ruins of an old barn. From this point the views to the north and west encompass Preston and the flat lands of the Fylde. Blackpool Tower is easily spotted whilst further to the north the concrete blocks mark Heysham nuclear power station. Clearer days will allow views to the southern peaks of the Lake District including Coniston Old Man, once Lancashire's highest point but since 1974 a part of Cumbria. Further to the east the long back of Longridge Fell leads towards the Pennines and the distinctive shape of Pendle Hill before the horizon disappears behind the near hilltop.

Pass to the left of the old barn and walk along the rough roadway to Pikelow Farm, entering the yard by one stile and leaving by another at the far end. Continue along the track, walking to the left of the row of white-painted cottages to reach a new housing development. Here turn left and walk a short distance uphill, looking on your right for the tarmaced footpath which cuts down between two housing estates. Go along this – you'll know if you've found the correct path as there are some old stone barns a little way down on the right – and follow it all the way downhill, crossing a new access road en route. Continue on down the road at the end to reach the old part of this, the village of Brinscall.

At the High Street turn left and walk to the bottom of the hill. Where the road bends sharp left continue straight on; to your right an old mill lodge now acts as the focal point of a large recreational area. Within a matter of yards turn right along Well Lane and look for the gate into the woodland on your right, just beside the derelict garage and rusting camper vans. Go through this gate and walk on into the woodlands.

Choice of route

This next section of the walk, whilst following a public right of way, involves a steep scramble at the head of a gorge. If you wish to avoid this then simply remain with Well Lane and wind uphill to the point where a fork occurs, the right hand track being gated off. Cross the stile beside this gate to rejoin the walk.

Once in the woodland, Wheelton Plantation, follow the obvious path through the largely birch trees to reach a swift flowing stream. Turn left and work your way up alongside it, the route is not obvious, just take the line of least resistance through the trees and up the steepening gradient. In a short while you'll come to the foot of a waterfall tumbling over the lip of a long deserted quarry now festooned with mosses, ferns and trees, altogether a very picturesque spot. You need now to scramble to the top of the quarry. I found that the best route was well to the left of the waterfall, up a steep but distinct path beneath some tall fir trees. This brings you to a fence alongside the gate mentioned in the choice of route, above. Climb over the fence – I couldn't find a stile – and turn right to cross the bridge over the stream just above the waterfall, following the track round to the right and down into the woodlands.

Remain with this track all the way through the plantation, ignoring side paths off to the right. The birch are now largely supplanted by mature oak and beech woodland, dotted with sycamore and conifers. In season watch out – or listen – for jays and woodpeckers; some trees support enormous bracket fungi. At a number of sites you'll notice ruins and tumbled piles of dressed stone amongst the trees. These are the ruins of a calico print works and of the once locally important cottage industry of handloom weaving, largely extinct by the turn of the last century.

There's only one fork along the track, near to some of these ruins; keep right here. Some way later a track joins from the left. On leaving the woods cross the stile to your right (i.e. not the one leading onto the moorland) and walk across the bridge over The Goit, an artificial watercourse and part of the immense system of reservoirs and feeder channels in the Anglezarke area. Continue along the track ahead, eventually crossing the bridge over the old Chorley to Blackburn railway. Turn left along the road, then right having crossed the concrete bridge across a brook. Turn left immediately before the house and follow the track uphill to the right of the cottage on the hillside. At the end of the track cross the stile beside the gate and then follow the fence uphill, continuing straight up across the hillside by line of sight once the fence ends.

At the top left corner of the field you'll reach the site of a drained pond. Some fifty yards to the right of this cross the rickety stile and follow the line of the fence in front of you. There are immense views to the left across Chorley and the Lancashire Plain to the Great Orme and the mountains of Snowdonia. Cross the stile ahead and walk to the wooden building in the farmyard graced with a notice "Danger, Sheep Dip." The way now is left, through the paddock and across the line of three stiles in quick succession, the first leading to a narrow footbridge, the others on either side of a driveway. Once over the third stile go half left and then follow the holly hedge on your right round the corner and to the narrow end of the field. The stile here is partially blocked by a wire mesh fence and marked by an old stone gatepost. Cross this and walk ahead across the field, passing the wrecked vehicles to your left. On gaining the farm drive turn right and walk up to Briars Brow, turning left down the road to return to the Dressers Arms.

5. THE WEST PENNINES: RILEY GREEN

Route: Riley Green – Darwen Gorge – Close Farm – Pleasington

Distance: 7 Miles

Map: Sheet SD 62/72 Blackburn

Start: The Royal Oak Hotel, Riley Green

Access: The hamlet of Riley Green is on the A675 Preston to Bolton road about six miles southeast of Preston and also off the A674 about three miles west of Blackburn. From Preston take the A675 towards Bolton through Higher Walton and Hoghton. On reaching Riley Green the pub is on the left just past the junction of the A675 with the A6061 beside which road the pub stands. From Blackburn take the A674 road towards Chorley and Preston and turn right along the A6061 at the sign to Preston, the pub is about a mile along on the right.

By rail you can join the walk at Pleasington Station which is on the Preston to Blackburn/Colne line and has a daily service, hourly Mondays to Saturdays, every two hours on Sundays.

The Royal Oak Hotel (0254 201445)

Until 1980 the Royal Oak was a part of the Estate of nearby Hoghton Tower and had served Estate workers since becoming a pub in 1711. Up to 1901 the driveway to the fortified manor house left the turnpike road beside the pub. It was originally a farm and the farmyard survived until the 1950's when the building was extended using Estate elm wood; the room to your right as you face the bar was the farmyard. Since 1980 the pub has been supplied with mild and bitter by Daniel Thwaites of nearby Blackburn, kept in exemplary fashion by landlord John Sansome whose beer keeping skills have been recognised by the award of Membership of the British Institute of Innkeeping, a sought-after trade accolade.

Its a very popular pub both with locals, with travellers from nearby Blackburn, Preston and Chorley and boaters from the canal. Apart from the beer one thing that appeals is the absence of any fruit machines, juke box or background music. John has a passion for steam engines; one of the several distinct areas of the long, low, heavily beamed pub houses a display of model engines which he himself built. You can call on bar meals each lunchtime between noon to 2 pm and also on Wednesday to Sunday evenings from 7 pm to 9.30 pm. The Thwaites ales may be quaffed between 11 am to 3 pm and 5.30 pm to 11 pm. The Royal Oak is well known to local rambling clubs who often use it as a base for their walks so as a reader of this book you're assured of a genuinely warm welcome.

Hoghton Tower

Half a mile due north (ie behind) of the Royal Oak is the sixteenth century fortified manor house of Hoghton Tower, home, since it was built, to the de Hoghton family. From many angles the house is difficult to see, being built on a heavily wooded hilltop site; certainly from this walk you will see little more than tantalizing glimpses of the building. It's worth going to see as a leading example of its genre, a footpath leads from beside the pub to the driveway leading up to the house, a half mile stroll across gently rising fields. Past visitors included King James the First in 1617; so impressed was he by the repast provided for him by the de Hoghton family of the day that, as the well known story goes, he "Knighted" a loin of beef (presumably for services to the royal palate) since which time that particular cut of beef has been known as sirloin. The family fared rather less well as the monarch's lengthy stay essentially bankrupted them. The Tower is open to the public each Sunday from Easter to the end of October and also on Saturdays in July and August.

The Walk

Turn left from the Royal Oak and walk along the busy A6061 for about two hundred yards to reach a farm drive on the left, marked by two cream painted gateposts and virtually opposite a red brick house. Go along this drive to the point where it hairpins to the left, at which point you should go through the gate-stile on your right (next to the field gate) and follow the sunken track down across the field, heading for the woods and the steep valley side. Cross a further stile, continue downhill to the end of the wire fence on your left and then carefully work your way down to the riverside. Walk downstream with this, the River

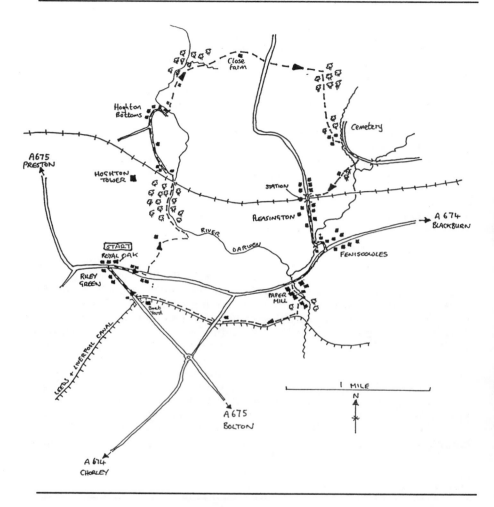

Darwen, entering the wooded gorge via a stile. For the next half mile or so simply follow this riverside path, crossing footbridges and side streams as necessary.

The gorge is rich in flora and fauna. In season great tracts of wild balsam, willowherb and butterbur blanket the banks of the Darwen. This river is cleaner than it at first may appear, evidenced by the occasional glimpse of a kingfisher and the large number of dipper, heron, ducks and coots, none of which species tolerate polluted water for long. At the weir the old mill leat splits off to the left, the footpath follows a wide track between this and the deepening gorge, particularly impressive when the river is in spate with a series of rapids, shoots and whirlpools. Pass beneath the viaduct carrying the Preston to Blackburn/Colne railway over a hundred feet above the water and then follow the path away from the river, across a footbridge and past the site of one of the old mills which once provided employment for several hundred in the area; some cottages and the mill house remain standing.

Remain with the metalled road – Viaduct Road – you have now joined and at the end turn right to walk downhill into the hamlet of Hoghton Bottoms. Curve round right with the road and walk to the last cottage on the left. Immediately past this turn left and cross the River Darwen on the green footbridge. From the bridge walk straight ahead, cross the low wooden stile and walk up past the stone barn and attached farmhouse. Wind round the end of this to cross a further stile, having crossed which remain with the hedge to your left.

In a short while pass the scout hut to your right and then follow the track up around the hillside, leaving the river to carve its way through a second gorge. Looking back from this track the chimneys of Hoghton Tower are visible standing above the trees. Remain with the woodland edge, crossing the first small brook and continuing the long, steady climb away from the river. At the top, and about fifteen yards before the track crosses a second brook and bends sharply left, climb up to your right and look for the track ahead and to your left, easily identified by the sharp, red earth bank on its right. Walk along this track for a short way, entering the area of trees. The obvious gap in the line of trees to the left marks the point where a stream has been culverted. Cross here and walk straight up the grassy slope ahead of you to a stile in the wall on the ridge crest. Cross this and rest awhile to take in the extensive views to your left (north) which stretch over Preston and well up into the Forest of Bowland and to Kirkby Fell in the Yorkshire Dales. Your route lies straight ahead, aim for the stone farm building on the near horizon, Close Farm.

Leave the field by the stile to the left of the gate into the farmyard and walk through the small, rough pasture, leaving by the broken gate next to the old bath tub. At the subsequent gap in the wall turn right, bringing you to the entrance to Close Farm, marked by a cattle grid. Opposite you is a small stile at the point where the wire fence meets the thorn hedge; the legend "public footpath" is faintly painted on it in blue paint. Cross this and follow the line of the garden fence up the field.

Where this turns right you turn half right, pass through one of the gaps in the threadbare hedge and turn left, following the line of this hedge, then the next one. You'll pass by a small circular walled enclosure en route, this is a small reservoir. At the far end of the second field go through the gate, cross directly over the minor road and walk along the driveway opposite towards Maiden House Farm. From this point you can pick out the Ribble estuary beyond Preston and distant views over the Fylde coast to the Lake District.

Where the drive bears right continue straight ahead and follow the line of hedge. Pass through the narrow stile by the gate and head straight across the field, leaving via the old gate by the holly tree. From here follow the line of trees across the next field, heading for the obvious wooden stile ahead of you, its position marked by a short section of plank fencing in the boundary hedge. Cross this stile and walk up the slight bank into the woods. After only a few yards join the main path and turn right in front of a silver birch tree, then walking gradually downhill. At the fork bear right and continue downhill, joining the line of a wall on your left. These woodlands are dotted with the well overgrown remains of small quarries, once worked for millstone grit building blocks.

At the end of the track leave the woods via the steep stile and head straight down the large field, using the horizon-dominating transmitter which tops Winter Hill as a line of travel. Some way off to your left is Witton Park, a massive area of public parkland owned by Blackburn Borough Council. At the foot of the field (ignoring the remains of a hedge through which you've passed) you should walk down a sunken track which leads to the right of a small hangar of beech trees. Scramble up then to the path which runs along the bank to the right of the track, now host to a stream. Climb the stile – the footings of which are cross sections of a felled tree – and walk down to the surfaced road. Turn right along this, passing between new houses and an old barn, and walk along for about fifty yards. At the corner you should turn left in front of some red brick houses. The actual footpath is immediately to this side of the gardens of these houses but is overgrown; local practice is to pass through the ruined metal gates and walk along the old driveway leading into the grounds of Pleasington Old Hall. After about fifty yards follow the path off to the right along a line of tall fir trees to end up on a surfaced road serving the local cemetery. Turn right down this and walk down to and through the gates at the bottom.

Once through these gates bear right along the rough road running behind the sports field, crossing the stream to your right where it is culverted about thirty yards along. Virtually immediately look forwards and to the right. You'll see a footpath leading past an upright stile and into a narrow cleft. Before reaching the stile a track branches left and winds uphill, fir trees to its left, a wall to its right. This is the route you should now follow, winding up the hillside to the old farm at the top. Cross the stile to enter the old yard of Tonguehill Farm which dates from 1735. Ahead you'll see a footpath sign directing you left between two fallen barns. Cross the stile into the pasture here and then follow the line of stiles virtually straight ahead, ending up at a gate giving you access to a narrow path which parallels the railway line. Walk along this path to its end and turn left along the road at the top. Pleasington station is down to your right whilst on the left is the Railway pub which sells Wilsons and Websters beers. Simply remain with the road, here called Victoria Road, for the next half mile, passing between late Victorian villas and earlier gritstone farm buildings. Wind across Walk Mill Bridge at the bottom (the mill burned down in 1864) and pass the picturesque, squat, Immanuel church, then walk steeply uphill to reach the busy A674 road.

Turn right and walk downhill. In the gorge to your right are the remains of several old mills, one mill house dating from 1830 survives. After about a third of a mile pass by the entrance to the Sun Paper Mill on your left and then cross the bridge over a deeply incised stream. Cross the road here and walk down the road into the paper mill complex. Walk along with the works on your right and the stream on your left until you come to the second security barrier (yes, it is a public right of way). Pass this second barrier (there's a security lodge on the left) and turn immediately right. You'll know if you're in the right spot if the building on your right is painted blue and that on your left is built of prefabricated panelling. Walk up the hillside, joining the obvious footpath after thirty yards or so, and wind on up through the woods. At the top is the tow-path of the Leeds & Liverpool Canal. Turn right along this, the water to your left. The justification for including this walk in the West Pennines is here, the canal acts as the border to the immense recreational area at this point. Remain with the tow-path for a little over a mile to reach a boatyard on the opposite bank. Leave the tow-path at the bridge here, turn right and walk up along the road back to the Royal Oak which is a few yards to the right from the junction at the end.

6. THE FOREST OF BOWLAND: OAKENCLOUGH

Route: Oakenclough – Grizedale – Barnacre – Calder Vale

Distance: 8 Miles

Map: Sheet SD 44/54 Garstang

Start: The Moorcock Inn, Oakenclough

Access: The hamlet of Oakenclough is an isolated community about four miles east of Garstang. Head south from Garstang along the B6430 for about a mile to Bowgreave where a narrow road on the left is signposted to Oakenclough and Calder Vale. Go down here, cross the motorway bridge and bear left, then follow the signs to Oakenclough. When you reach the junction opposite the mill at the hamlet turn right; the Moorcock is then about half a mile uphill on the left.

The Moorcock Inn (09952 2130)

Standing in isolated splendour on the edge of Bleasdale Moors, it is obvious that the pub was once a farm. Typical of the Pennines, the farmhouse and barn were all part of the same building, the barn has simply been converted into a third bar and function room. The building itself dates back over three hundred years but no one can hazard a guess as to when it first became a pub, one of the highest and most isolated in Lancashire

This isolation gives it a certain fame and it's a popular spot, particularly in the summer, for trippers from the coastal resorts on the Fylde. Their diligence in making the trip is amply rewarded by the choice of handpumped Tetley's Mild and Bitter, Ind Coope Burton Ale (CAMRA Beer of the Year in 1990) and the pub's own label Moorcock Bitter; which brewery produces this tasty pint is a secret the landlord is unwilling to share. Of the three bars, two are in daily use, a large public bar with attendant pool table and darts board and a quieter, carpeted lounge complete with beams and, in winter, a roaring log fire. In a glass case behind the lounge bar a stuffed mink is making off with a Red Grouse chick; the pub's name is the nickname for a Red Grouse which are common on the high moors which rise steeply behind the pub.

There's a comprehensive range of bar snacks and meals available every day up to 2.45 at lunchtime and 9.45 at night; the Ploughman's lunch is exceptional value. Children are catered for with their own special "Flintstone's Menu." The pub itself is open from 11.30 am to 3 pm and 6.30 pm (7 pm in winter) to 11 pm.

THE FOREST OF BOWLAND

Bowland is one of the few remaining wilderness areas in England, a high swathe of the western edge of the Pennines characterised by immense tracts of moorland deeply dissected by gorge-like cloughs, well wooded in their lower sections where the becks and rivers spill out into more gentle but equally inspiring rolling countryside. The whole area was designated an Area of Outstanding Natural Beauty (AONB) in 1964, one step away from a National Park.

Virtually no roads penetrate the fastness of the high moors and fells. The only through road is a narrow, winding minor road that follows the chasm of a tributary of the River Hodder known widely as the Trough of Bowland; other roads or tracks peter out at isolated farmsteads or the gaunt ruins of shepherds' huts or old shooting lodges. Even footpaths and bridleways have only the most tenuous of holds in the area, these are essentially just a few old salters' ways or packhorse trails. One reason for this is that the area escaped virtually scot-free the attentions of even the most doughty Victorian quarrymen or water engineers. Thus whilst most areas of the Pennines are criss-crossed by tramway trackbeds, lead miners tracks, reservoir leats and quarry roads the sharp edges of the Bowland Fells acted as fortress walls and kept out the invaders.

Little can have changed since the Danes and Vikings, then the Normans, strove to turn the area to their advantage. It is the Normans we can thank for the name of the area. "Forest" refers not to a large, heavily wooded tract but to an area of exclusivity, a hunting area or Chase reserved for the use of the monarch or his earls and lords and subject to the often barbaric Forest Law of the day in place of the common law. An early holder of the title to the Bowland area was John of Gaunt. The last truly wild deer was killed in about 1805, the deer you may see or hear today – Red, Fallow, Roe, Sika or Muntjak are more recent introductions. This exclusivity to a large extent remains even to this day. Large areas of

Bowland are private shooting estates managed to ensure a good supply of grouse and to which access is jealously guarded, although a few areas of the peripheral Fells are available to walkers under access agreements made between Lancashire County Council and the landowners or water company.

THE WALK

(The section of walk beyond Sullom Side is very muddy after rain).

Leave the Inn, turn right and walk down the road to the small, scattered hamlet of Oakenclough, no more than a few farms and cottages and the large buildings of the old paper mill, now used by a number of small firms. Remain on the main road and walk uphill out of this valley of the River Calder. Views soon open up to the right along the Calder Valley and over the Bleasdale Moors whilst to your left are glimpses of Grizedale Lea Reservoir. Continue along the road, cross the cattle grid and then turn left along the signposted bridleway. Keep the wall immediately to your right, pass through the gate at the end and walk on round to the right, keeping the by-now broken wall on your right, to reach another gate. Once through this walk ahead along the line of the slightly sunken path across the field, heading towards a pylon on the middle horizon. Views from this point are extensive, north west beyond Lancaster to the mountains of the Lake District and west across the sweep of Morecambe Bay, the ever present moors to the east offering a sharp contrast.

Go through a further gate and walk along for a few yards with a brook on the left to reach a solid metal gate. Go through this and turn right to follow the line of the fence down to the farmyard at Fell End Farm. The way now is between the barns and up to the farmhouse; last time I was here the path was badly obstructed by gates, drums and barn doors, but persevere as this is a public bridleway. On reaching the farmhouse swing left and walk along the farm drive, crossing a brook and walking up the shallow rise ahead. At the top of this rise turn left along the bridleway signposted to Nicky Nook via Grizedale Valley and walk along with this towards the woodlands, entering these after crossing the Bailey Bridge.

Many walks in Lancashire offer unexpected surprises but this is surely one of the best. Follow the roadway down through the beech and oak woodlands thick with an undergrowth of rhododendrons resplendent in May and June, crossing bridges and gates as necessary. You soon reach

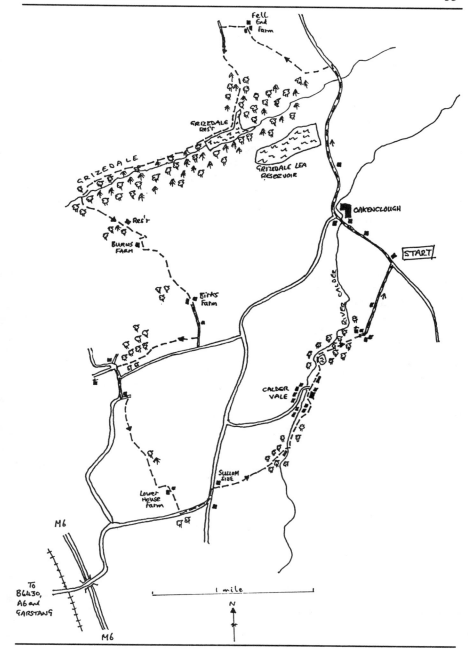

an arm of Grizedale Reservoir on your left and this remains with you for the next half mile or so. It's a glorious setting, the far, nearly vertical hillside thickly wooded with oak, beech and firs right to the waters edge whilst "your" hillside is carpeted with heather, bracken and bilberry bushes. Birdlife abounds here with a great variety of waterbirds, birds of prey and smaller woodland species.

Go through the gate beside the dam, ignore the track that angles up the hillside and walk down the valley, the Grizedale Brook winding its course far below you on your left. Remain with the path for about a mile, soon working down to the level of the brook, darting in and out of the trees and crossing a footbridge across a side stream. You'll eventually reach a gate leading into pastureland beyond the woods. Once through this gate look to your left for a footbridge across the Grizedale Brook, the adjoining signpost pointing the direction to Burns Farm. Cross the footbridge and walk up the path for a few yards only, then double back on yourself steeply uphill to reach a stile marked with two white-painted arrows. Cross the stile and walk up the steep path through the woodlands following the white arrows to the stile at the top. From here walk across the field in the direction that the arrow points to the ridge top and from this point walk towards the domes of light coloured corrugated sheeting half hidden by trees some distance ahead, crossing a brook to reach these.

The corrugated sheets cover a small reservoir; walk along the access road, bear right at the end and then almost immediately left along the drive to Burns Farm. Walk on through to the far end of the farmyard and bear left up the track, winding round to the right and climbing gradually uphill. At the point where the track turns sharply left continue straight ahead, cross the stile to the right of the gate and follow the edge of the field straight ahead. Continue across the fields towards Birks Farm, cross the stream via the bridge and walk up with the farm track through the farmyard. Beyond the farmyard follow the driveway, curving right by the red-roofed barn. About 120 yards or so beyond here look to your right to find a stile in the wooden rail fence. Cross this and walk ahead down the field to a further stile between two oak trees beside a little pond. Once over this stile walk down the line of the decrepit hedge to a further stile beside a gate at the end of this long pasture; cross this and head half left for the corner of the woodlands ahead, then following the woodland edge down to the minor road.

Turn left along the road and follow it to the sharp right bend, here turning left up the drive beside the red-doored lodge house. In just a few yards is a stile below some willow trees on your right, cross this and walk across the fields ahead, crossing several more stiles and always keeping the fence/hedge just to your left. Cross the stream and bear half left up the subsequent field, then looking for a stile beneath an oak tree on the right; once over this walk left up the muddy track, climb the gate at the end and turn right to walk through the farmyard of Lower House Farm, continuing along its driveway to the minor road at the far end.

Turn left and walk up the road, bear left at the top and walk along to the first farm on the right, Sullom Side. Turn right up along the short drive and pass through the gate ahead, the farm to your left. Once through the gate follow the track beyond up the hillside. At the end of the track go through the left hand gate and then walk downhill with the wire fence immediately on your right to reach a stile into the woodlands at the bottom. Follow the track down through the woods to reach the River Calder again at the site of an old mill, Low Mill. The mill itself was demolished in the 1960's but the site of the old header reservoirs can still be seen in the woods up to your left. The mill marks the south end of the hamlet of Calder Vale. Pass by the terrace of cottages to your right and then immediately take the path down to the footbridge across the Calder in a delightful rapids-strewn wooded glade.

Calder Vale Millpond

Turn left off the footbridge and follow the river upstream, the path is boggy in places where springs issue from the steep hillside. The main part of the hamlet soon comes into view up to the left across the river. Walk across the pasture you reach and go through the gate between the barns some yards up from the river. Wind along between the barns, pass the farmhouse on your left and then walk alongside the massive wall of Lappet Mill which still produces textiles in this hidden and isolated spot.

On reaching the bridge you're in the centre of Calder Vale and can see virtually every building. The terraces were provided by the mill owners; there were once four shops but now only a post office stores remains. The mill owners were Quakers, the workers largely Methodists, both of which explain the lack of a village pub although there was apparently once a Temperance Hotel. It's worth spending some time exploring this fascinating surviving mill hamlet before continuing.

The way out of the hamlet lies on the same side of the river as the mill. Walk up past the Methodist Chapel and along the front of Long Row terrace, at the end passing through the gate and walking along to the old mill lodge. Walk on with this lake on your right and follow the surfaced path on up through the woods. This path is well maintained for a purpose, it leads up to the church of St. John which is in an isolated woodland setting half way between Calder Vale and Oakenclough, both of which it serves. Walk past the church and neighbouring junior school, follow the road round to the left and walk the remaining half mile back to the Moorcock Inn.

Only get caught short in Calder Vale at the weekend!

7. THE FOREST OF BOWLAND: CHIPPING

Route: Chipping – Knot Hill – Greystoneley – Dinkling Green – Birchen Lee

Distance: 9 Miles

Map: Sheet SD 64/74 Clitheroe and Chipping

Start: The Sun Inn, Chipping

Access: Chipping is about 5 miles north of Longridge at the centre of a complex web of unclassified minor roads. It is, however, well signposted from Longridge which is, itself, about 7 miles north-east of Preston along the B6243. Park in the free car park in the village centre.

The Sun Inn (0995 61206)

The Inn stands in a commanding position right at the heart of Chipping at the junction of Windy Street and Talbot Street, looking down the steep slope of the latter over the village's two other pubs and post office to the old corn mill on Chipping Brook, now a restaurant. Even this lofty perch wasn't enough for the builders in 1758 – the front door is only accessible up a considerable flight of stone steps.

It's well worth the climb, however (and for exhausted ramblers the back door is step-less), as the Sun is everything you'd expect of a village local. It's a relief to be able to say this, as the hand of Boddington – or, at least, their design and development section – recently touched the pub. Many a local has been gutted and changed beyond all recognition during the last decade or so through such a touch but thankfully, in the case of The Sun, little more than cosmetic surgery was applied. The tiny old central bar remains intact, a serving hatch supplies the entrance passageway and games room whilst the main bar serves the locals snug. A new room creates a comfortable extension to this snug (it was the kitchen) whilst a fourth room abuts the games room and passageway.

The whole pub was redecorated and simply but comfortably furnished in time for landlord Wilf Blezard to take over in September 1990. A bit of a globetrotter, Wilf moved all of 100 yards up from The Talbot Inn where he'd spent 15 years perfecting the art of keeping Boddingtons Mild and Bitter, both of which slip down a treat at The Sun. Maybe he's helped by the ambient temperature maintained in the cellar by a stream which is culverted beneath but which floods the cellar in times of heavy rain on the surrounding moors. "Guest" beers have been tried in the past but local and visitor alike find that Wilf's Boddingtons is something special, so guest beers are superfluous.

The pub started life as a farm; the range of outbuildings behind the pub remain from those days and are due to be converted by the brewery into craft shops. When it became a pub no-one is quite sure. It was certainly one in 1835, however. In that year nineteen year old Elizabeth Dean was due to be married on November 5th. Taking a "stiffener" in The Sun before the ceremony she happened to glance across the road to the neighbouring church only to see her betrothed entering the churchyard to marry another. The distraught Elizabeth took herself to the pub's attic there to hang herself; her ghost is said to haunt the pub, her simple gravestone stands next to the old yew in the churchyard.

The Sun is open from 11 am to 4 pm and 6 am to 11 pm Mondays to Fridays and usually all day on Saturdays. If the excellent beer is not enough to fill the gap then either pie and peas or a sandwich should do the trick.

Chipping

The tight knit village community can trace a history going back at least a thousand years. The word Chipping is derived from the Old English name for market, much more common in the West Country where towns famous for their wool markets – Chipping Campden, Chipping Norton – still prosper. This Chipping grew largely as a market to disperse the sheep and woollen products derived from the moorland pastures of the Forest of Bowland, immediately north of the village and sweeping down to the east and west; a sheep fair and sales is still held in September.

The parish church of St. Bartholomew originated in the Tenth century. Although much altered in Victorian times it retains its solid, squat tower, medieval font and stonework purported to be Saxon in origin; the old yew in the churchyard is said to be as old as the foundation. John Wesley preached at the church twice, the second time the parishioners rebelled against his interpretation of the scriptures and sent him packing;

the incumbent rector, John Milner, travelled with him for a short time before returning to his sinecure at Chipping.

St Bartholomews, Chipping

The village itself is largely of seventeenth and eighteenth century buildings with some more recent developments to the west and along Windy Lane on the site of an old brass foundry. There were once eight mills in the village producing goods as diverse as spindles and corn. Only one now survives as a working concern; the old Kirk Mill was once a cotton mill but now produces the chairs for which the village (and the manufacturers H.J. Berry) is famous. The walk passes this works tucked away in the deep clough of Chipping Brook north west of the church. Here also is the old village workhouse, now a row of cottages. The village school and almshouses date from the 1600's and result from the benevolence of a local mill owner, John Brabin, who made his fortune from local wool; these buildings are in Windy Street. Chipping remains a thriving local centre catering for the local agricultural community, the needs of the chair works, a growing number of tourists and as a commuting settlement for Preston. All this and virtually unspoilt to-boot, a combination to savour.

The Walk

(Several shallow fords and streams need to be crossed on this walk)

Walk down Talbot Street from the Sun, passing the other two village pubs (The Talbot and the Tillotsons Arms both of which sell traditional ales) and cross Chipping Brook – look to your right to see the old corn mill and wheel, now a restaurant. Turn left at the war memorial along the road signposted for Dunsop Bridge and Bowland with Leagram and remain with it for about half a mile, passing an old estate lodge on your left. At the next turn to your left, which is the drive up to Leagram Hall, cross the cattle grid and wind up the drive through the parkland. When the woodland plantation is joined on your left continue up the drive to a point about half way up the woodland and then look to your right, just before reaching the oak tree nearest to the road on your right. Across the field beyond this (and slightly to the right) is a small plantation, uphill from which is an isolated oak. Leave the drive here and walk across the parkland to pass to the left of this isolated tree.

Once past the tree you'll come to a stile over the wire fence. Cross this and then walk ahead, keeping the fence and/or hedge on your left. Views to your right take in the end of Longridge Fell and, further away, the distinctive shape of Pendle Hill, to your left are the high fells of Bowland. Remain with the fence/hedge and cross two stiles and a brook. You'll then need to ford or jump across the mill leat leading to Leagram Mill, then cross a rickety footbridge over Leagram Brook. Once across turn half left and walk uphill out of the trees. Cross the stiles at the top and then walk across the field aiming for the left hand side of the knoll ahead, Knot Hill. Simply walk around this limestone knoll which has been partially quarried away on its northern side; the workings are well overgrown. Look on your right for the semi-circular entrance to an old limekiln; this is where much of the quarried limestone will have ended up being roasted to provide lime for use to break down clayey soils or to be used as a base for whitewash.

Walk around to join the farm drive by the isolated Knot Barn and turn left along it, walking along to Lower Greystoneley, recently rebuilt, and through the farmyard. Go through the gate at the far end and walk downhill along the deteriorating track into the woods. At the ford look to the left to find a footbridge over Greystoneley Brook and then rejoin the track and walk up the far bank. Pass through the gate at the top and walk along to the farmhouse at Upper Greystoneley, passing between

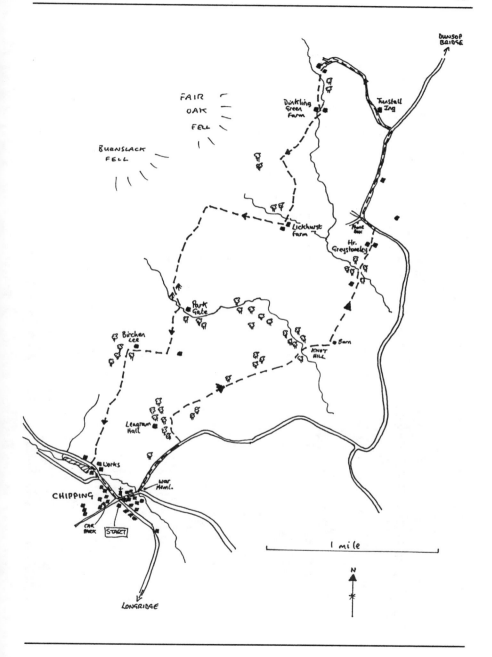

this on your left and the barns on your right. Remain with the driveway to reach a minor road and turn left along this, following it for the next mile or so, bearing sharp right after a short distance at the corner near the telephone box at the sign to Dunsop Bridge.

Walk up the hill through the knolly limestone area, pass beneath the line of electricity cables and about 150 yards later turn left along the minor road to Tunstall Ing; there's also a no through road sign and a cattle grid here. Walk on past the cottage and up around the end of the hillocks known as Long Knots; off to your right are extensive views over the beautiful Hodder Valley and up towards Gisburn Forest and the high moors and Dales of North Yorkshire. The graceful bridge across the Hodder is Burholme Bridge. Where the road forks keep left and walk down to the farm. Go through the gate into the yard and bear right, passing in front of the farmhouse and walking down the yard to the gate beside the bull pen. Go through this gate, down the track and across the footbridge beside the ford. Walk up the valley side opposite to a point just beyond the poultry houses but before the fence and turn left, walking along with the rail fence on your right. After 100 yards or so

Knot Hill and Fair Oak Fell

look for the steep stile on the right across the fence just where a gap in the line of trees appears. Cross this and aim for Dinkling Green Farm in the distance, crossing a further stile en route about 25 yards to the right of the gate in the fence.

Aim to enter the farmyard between the house on your right and the barn on the left, walking down a short ginnel to the farmyard. Continue on through the yard to the black gate on the right between two buildings, going through this and down the lane beyond. Walk through the long, shallow ford and carry on up the rough track beyond, remaining with it for about 150 yards. Bear left at your end of the narrow band of immature woodland, pass through the gate at the end and follow the line of fence on your right. This is a good area to watch buzzard in action, sweeping effortlessly on their enormous wings across the lower slopes of Burnslack and Fair Oak Fells, their occasional plaintive "mewing" call breaking the still air of a summers day.

Go through the gate at the bottom and up the slope beyond, keeping the stream on your left to reach the gate on the corner at the top. Pass

Moorland track above Lickhurst Farm

through this and walk along the edge of this field to the stone gateposts, go through these and head slightly right to the gate in the wall ahead. From here simply walk straight ahead and down into the deep, narrow valley ahead, aiming for the farm on the far side. Cross the stile to the left of the boggy area and walk down to the stream, walk over the footbridge and up the drive to Lickhurst Farm.

Bear right just before the buildings and go along the edge of the yard, following the track for about thirty yards and pass through the gate straight ahead of you, joining a rutted track leading towards the fells (if you get to the gate beside the poultry house you've gone just too far). Amble along this track, an old quarry road, for about half a mile to the point where it curves left and splits. Take the track virtually straight ahead – the one that passes through a shallow cutting – and once through the cutting angle gradually left away from the track and up onto the moor, aiming to walk just below the right hand side of the summit of the hill on your left. Once here look for the tall Scots Pines and walk down to these. Far beyond you can see Longridge church spire and, beyond this, Preston.

You'll reach the nearest of these pine trees at the corner of two walls. Your route here is through the rickety gate and down past the fallen tree to the stream at the bottom. You'll need to ford this then walk up the other bank to join the farm driveway from Park Gate Farm. Walk up the drive away from the farm and remain with it until the junction with a concreted drive nearly half a mile on. At this point, marked by an old milk churn stand, turn right and walk along to Birchen Lee Farm. Walk on past the farmhouse and through the small yard, turning left through the gate immediately through the yard and before you reach the stream. Follow the fence on the left, cross the brook at the end and then aim for the trees in the corner of the field ahead of you, in line with Longridge church spire. Cross the stile at this point, pass by the small overgrown quarry workings to your right and join the obvious track that comes up out of the deep valley of Dobson's Brook.

Follow this track left, heading towards Chipping which is now visible some distance ahead. Climb the stile and remain to the right of the ditch and fence, walking gradually downhill to the millpond. Cross the stile a few yards up the driveway of the big house on the right and walk left down the drive to the minor road, turning left along this. The millpond is that which fed the Kirk Cotton Mill, now a chair works. The road winds through the works and past the old three storey workhouse; bear left at the top to return to the village centre.

8. THE FOREST OF BOWLAND: WHITEWELL

Route: Whitewell – Crimpton – Browsholme – Middle Lees

Distance: 6 Miles

Map: Sheet SD 64/74 Clitheroe and Chipping

Start: The Inn at Whitewell

Access: The easiest way to find Whitewell is to start from Whalley, just south of Clitheroe and off the A59. Whitewell is signposted from Whalley, turn left along Station Road towards Mitton and then simply follow the signs for Whitewell and the Trough of Bowland through the maze of back roads for about eight miles.

The Inn at Whitewell (02008 222)

Whitewell is The Inn. A handful of cottages, a chapel and a farm about half a mile to the north are all that keep this idyllic rural retreat company. Perched above a bend of the River Hodder this venerable inn – parts of which are over five hundred years old – commands the ages old route along the valley at a point where the river plunges headlong from a wide fertile plain into a deep, winding, wooded gorge, guarded at this northern end by the wooded dome of New Laund Hill. Nestling by the hotel, the tiny Georgian St Michaels Church was completely rebuilt in 1817.

Eulogies about the Hotel, of which the Inn is an integral part, can be found in virtually every hotel guide, touring guide or pub guide, be it in English, American, German or Japanese. I won't deign to add to these; suffice to say that the hotel is virtually peerless for food and for the range of wines – over 140 – on offer and the world beats a path to its door. Perhaps surprisingly, this doesn't mean that the Inn is terminally crowded or expensive. Quite the contrary, in fact, the pub itself is a modest and convivial establishment catering for a wide variety of users from the "Huntin', Shootin' and Fishin'" fraternity – the Hotel has a six mile stretch of the river's salmon and trout rights and entertains shooting parties at local farms – to ramblers and local farmers and has a brisk passing trade.

This mixed bag of clientele are entertained in the "Coffee Room" if you go by the evidence of the frosted glass in the front door which draws you into the cosy bar area. Heavily-leaded stone-mullioned windows help light the main room which has a welcoming open log fire as its centre-piece and is simply furnished with a pot-pourri of oak chairs, tables and settles on a carpeted flagstoned floor. Old prints decorate the walls which also sport the obligatory stuffed fox heads and a case of stuffed owls and birds of prey. For any self-respecting reader of this book, however, a glance at the bar is rewarded by the sight of handpumps dispensing the excellent products of Moorhouses' Burnley Brewery, their Premier Bitter and the renowned but strong Pendle Witches Brew which should be handled with care. A glance through the bar reveals a games room with pool, darts, shove ha'penny and the like whilst adjoining the main room is a lounge area with another roaring fire, a baby grand piano, longcase clock, settles and a small library of local interest books.

Proprietor Richard Bowman offers a very varied bar meals menu which includes such gems as Bangers Vin Rouge, Vegetable Crumble and Gourmet Fishermans Pie; bar meals are available from noon to 2 pm and 7.30 pm to 9.30 pm, the Inn itself is open between 11 am to 3 pm and 6 pm to 11 pm and children are welcome.

The Walk

Start up the narrow road opposite the hotel, bear left and in a few yards look on the right for a flight of steps climbing up to a gate. Pass through this gate and walk up the field aiming for the lone cottage ahead with the cream painted side wall, Seed Hill. The actual right of way is to turn left and walk behind the cottage, then following the line of bushes and trees uphill and on your right although the evidence is that many walkers walk up in front of the cottage to join this old hedgerow. Once at the top of the field go through the gate and angle slightly to the left, aiming for the obvious gate in the wall to the left of the limestone knoll at the top end of this field. On your right beside this gate is the rounded mouth of an old lime kiln where rock quarried from the knoll was roasted. Look carefully at the blocks of stone which make up the dry stone wall by the gate, they're full of fossils, largely Crinoids, a now-extinct kind of long stemmed sea-lily distantly related to starfish.

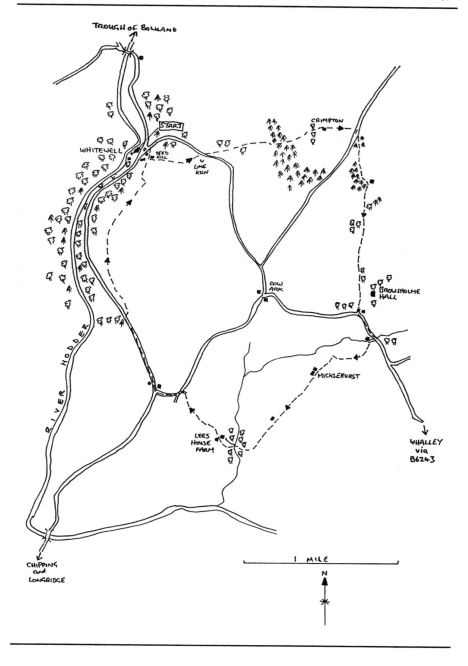

The Inn at Whitewell

Behind you are extensive views across the Hodder valley to Mellor Knoll and Totridge Fell, at over 1600 feet one of Bowland's highest points.

Cross straight over the narrow road here and go through the gate opposite. Bear right and walk along the track for a short while, leaving it before it bends left to find the ladder stile over the wall ahead. Once over this walk up to the isolated group of trees in the pasture ahead. These are growing round a series of pot-holes and natural sinks in the porous limestone at this spot. Pass to the left of these trees and then bear slightly right and walk ahead across the rough pasture, up to the right of the shallow valley. On reaching the wall at the far end look for the narrow but obvious gap through the thick plantation of evergreens on the other side of this wall, it is about a hundred yards up from the corner; the way over the wall is a rough stone step stile opposite this gap. Walk through the woods and, on emerging from such, go over the stile on the left and then head across the field to the line of trees at the far side. Pass through this line via the two gates and walk on to the farm, Crimpton, following the waymark arrows through the farmyard and walking on to the minor road at the end of the drive.

Turn right at the end and take a few paces uphill, looking on your left for the small stile beside the stump of an old telegraph pole. Climb this stile and then walk to your right uphill along the obvious line up the recently established coniferous plantation. At the top of the plantation cross the stile and turn left to follow the fence to the corner of the trees. From here walk up the field heading for the chimneys which poke just above the ridge top. Cross the track at the top and walk to the corner of the woodland near the cottage, going over the stile here (formed by two piles of stones concreted together) and then following the woodland edge. The cottage is dwarfed by a peculiar folly of a structure, reminiscent of a massive Tudor age chimney stack but evidently not functioning as such.

Turn right at the corner of the trees, cross another stone-pile stile and walk away from the cottage to the isolated brick shed. Turn your back on the woodland edge here and walk half right across the large field, aiming for the right hand edge of the loose area of beech trees which are, themselves, to the right of a conifer plantation; just head for the point where the line of telegraph poles leaves the field. At the far corner of these beech cross the stile beside the gate and turn right, walking to the far end of the pond on your left. From here walk down across the pasture to the left corner of the isolated spinney of fir and deciduous trees. Go down the track beside these trees and then look to the bottom end of the subsequent field to sight the track winding away from a series of gates. Walk down to this, cross the cattle grid and walk along this track to its end. Off in the trees to the left is Browsholme (pronounced brewzum) Hall, ancestral home of the Parker family and open to the public at various times of the year. At the bottom of the track go through the gate and walk on to the minor road at the sharp corner beside the lodge house. Bear left along the road and walk downhill to cross Mill Brook.

Immediately you've crossed the bridge go through the gate on your right, climb the steep bank up to the field and walk across it to the gate and stile in the fence opposite. The ridge dominating the horizon is Longridge Fell; behind you fleeting glimpses of Browsholme Hall in the woodlands. Turn right along the drive here and follow it round to Micklehurst Farm. Walk through the yard in front of the house, leaving by the gate at the far end and walk to the end of the pasture. Cross through the gate beside the stunted thorn tree here and join the track on your right which leads to the isolated Kinder Barn. Pass to the left of the barn and walk down the long field beyond, keeping to its right hand boundary. At the end go through the gate, turn right and go through the neighbouring gate into the steeply sloping pasture. Walk diagonally down the pasture, aiming to pass to the left of the large oak tree at the edge of the wooded valley bottom.

Work down the valley side to the stream and walk upstream to find and cross the new wooden footbridge. Such stalwart effort at providing this bridge is largely wasted by the complete lack of any waymarking or obvious path at the far side. You need to work up the steep wooded slope beyond, favouring your right hand and roughly following the line of the deep cleft off to the right – it really is a matter of following the line of least resistance. At the top of the bank you'll find yourself at Lees House Farm. The footpath here joins the farm's driveway, walk to your right through the farmyard and wind round with this driveway to the road at the end. Turn left and then sharp right with the surfaced road; the long straight trackway leaving at this sharp corner is the line of a Roman road from Ribchester. When you reach the junction turn right, following the sign for Whitewell, and remain with this road for about half a mile.

When you reach the arm of woodland on your left, go through the substantial black-painted metal gate on your right opposite the far corner of this woodland. Bear left and walk along the field virtually parallel with the road, aiming to go through the tall metal kissing gate beside the massive metal gate in the wall at the far end. Once through this walk ahead immediately below the small old quarry working and then follow the line of the wire fence around the contour, crossing stiles as and when necessary to reach a second tall kissing gate. Pass through this and look up to the right to the old quarry working which has exposed a nicely folded area of banded limestone. Walk on for a few yards to the field gate on the left. Go through this and then follow the old track beyond, winding round the hillside and slowly loosing height. The wisps of smoke curling up out of the valley ahead emanate from the Inn's chimneys; beyond this is an excellent view up the Hodder to the graceful Burholme Bridge. Walk down to the side of Seed Hill Cottage and then retrace the initial part of the walk to reach The Inn.

9. THE FOREST OF BOWLAND: SLAIDBURN

Route: Slaidburn – Burn House – Beatrix – Newton

Distance: 7 Miles

Map: Sheet SD 65/75 Slaidburn and Forest of Bowland

Start: The Hark to Bounty, Slaidburn

Access: Slaidburn is about nine miles to the north of Clitheroe on the B6478. From Clitheroe take the road to Waddington, thence climbing high over the moors to Newton where a right turn will bring you to Slaidburn about two miles further on. The Hark to Bounty is in the centre of the village close to the War Memorial. If you can't park at the pub then turn right at the sign to Settle and wind down to the car park near the river.

The Hark to Bounty (02006 246)

Having stooped to pass through the pub's low door your first impression may be that you've mistakenly walked into a restaurant, most of the tables in the long, low room having table cloths and appropriate condiments. Whilst justifiably proud of the excellent and unusual foods on offer (Roast Guinea Fowl or Venison, Rabbit and Pigeon Casserole for example), a glance ahead to the bar reveals that the fare offered by Marion and Brian Hough is certainly not at the expense of draught beers. A Scottish and Newcastle House, you've a choice of Theakstons Best Bitter and Old Peculiar, Youngers Bitter or Matthew Brown Mild all on handpump; the latter will no doubt disappear when Matthew Brown is closed down during 1991.

This is one of the most famous pubs in Lancashire, largely because of its unusual name. This dates back to 1875 when the local Squire was heard to remark to his drinking companions during a break from the Hunt, "Hark to Bounty," referring to the baying of his favourite foxhound which could be heard above the barking of its peers in the square outside. An unusual name although not unique, there are several "Hark to" pub names in the Bury area.

The pub itself dates back to the Thirteenth Century and for many years doubled as the local courthouse on the regular round of the travelling justices on the Lancaster to York Circuit. An external staircase still gives access to the first floor courtroom which was last used, for judicial purposes, in 1937. Nowadays the room is used to accommodate the overflow of customers during the summer months. In the winter one of the great draws of the pub is the splendid fire kept burning beneath its great copper chimneypiece, just a short step from the bar. The rest of the one large room is decorated with a restrained mix of brass and copper oddments.

Pub hours are noon to 3 pm and 6.30 pm to 11 pm during the Winter, all day during the summer (roughly May to September); the varied menu may be sampled in the winter months from noon to 2 pmand 6.30 pm to 9 pm; all day and evening in the summer. If you're captivated by the pub and the area (and it's hard not to be) then you can also stay at the Hark to Bounty.

Slaidburn

This is a gem of a village, little more than a cluster of cottages and farms huddled round a crossing of ways high up the Hodder valley. This crossroads has been there for aeons; some of the old salters roads across Bowland homed in on the place which, in consequence, developed as the administrative centre for the Forest of Bowland, hence the courtroom above the pub. Visually, hardly anything has changed over the centuries, as if the village had been mothballed. Virtually the only new building is a modest little health centre tucked away off one of the village roads; other "new" buildings include a poor-house by the green dating from 1852 and the nearby Methodist Chapel founded in 1821.

For the most part, however, the tiny sandstone cottages have looked at each other across the narrow streets and cobbled pavements for three or four hundred years. Some retain their solid external stairs and mounting blocks, harking back to the days when the upper storeys were used as haylofts and horses ruled the streets; the motor vehicle is an intruder here. Many of the storerooms and barns still remain in use amongst and alongside these cottages; no conversions or modernisations have been allowed, in all probability because much of the village belongs to one family with a great sense of tradition and propriety. One notable conversion has occurred, however; The Old Black Bull pub is now a Youth Hostel. Apart from upland farming – the name Slaidburn means "sheep field overlooking a river" – the villagers used to make a living from rearing rabbits, processing their pelts for use in the fur trade, or from working galena (lead) veins in the surrounding hills.

St. Andrew's Church, to the south of the village, is a Fifteenth Century rebuild of a much older structure; the list of Rectors goes back to 1246 but a pre-Norman foundation is likely. Inside are some fine box pews dating back to the 1600's, retaining the names of the families by which they were installed and used, and an unusual three-tier pulpit. There's also a beautifully carved wooden Chancel Screen dated 1634. Next to the churchyard stands the village Grammar School, endowed in 1717 and overflowing with tiny mullioned windows.

The Walk

Turn right out of the pub and walk down the hill, then wind gradually uphill out of the village. Down in the trees to the right are the remains of the old mill dam and leat, just upstream this Croasdale Beck winds through a tight wooded valley. Stay with this road for about a mile; it is very quiet as it doesn't lead to anywhere. Pass by Ellerbeck Hall, dating from 1694, on your left and walk up the hill beyond, turning left at the top along the driveway to Parrock Head Hotel and Restaurant. Walk through the car park in front of this converted farmhouse, go through the gate at the end and turn right before you get to the barn. Pass through the field gate and walk to the wall along the right of the field. Climb the stile at the top end of the field and remain with the wall on your right to the point where it bends right; from here walk across the field to the long, low, white building, Laythams.

Go through the gate to the right of the house and turn left along the road, then go through the rusty field gate on the right, opposite the middle of Laythams. Head half left across the field, aiming for the farm which is all but hidden in the left-hand fir plantation on the lower fell-side ahead. Cross the stile and walk to the corner of the fence ahead, walking along with this on your right for a short distance. Cross straight over the surfaced field track and a couple of brooks and walk across the rough pasture to the stile a few yards to the right of the short section of rail fencing. Climb this stile and walk to the wall on the left, walking uphill with this to the stone step stile protected by some wooden rail fence. Look at the stones in the wall beside this stile, some of them are limestone rich in fossils, mostly Crinoids but also corals and shells. Once

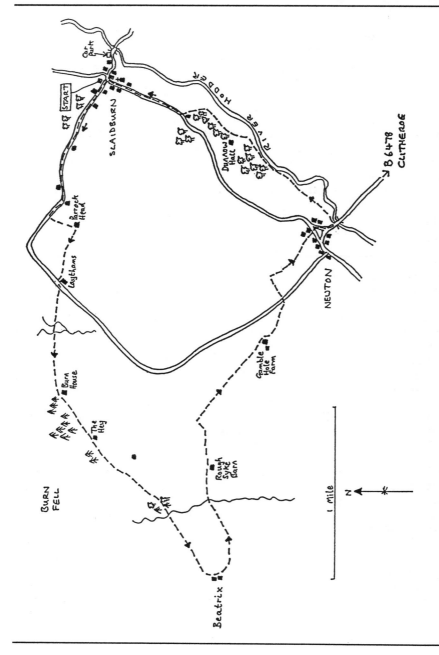

over this head across the field towards the fir trees just behind Burn House. Gain the roadway and follow it along behind the farm, then remaining with it for a good half mile, passing behind a further moorland edge house, The Hey.

The prospect from the road here is excellent. To your right the long line of Burn Fell, ahead a veritable family of fell tops above Dunsop Bridge culminating in Totridge Fell, one of the highest in the Forest of Bowland. Off to the left is limestone country; Rough Syke Beck in the valley below marks the approximate boundary between the gritstones and limestones in this part of Bowland, down the valley is the small, sharp knoll known locally as the Sugar Loaf. This varied landscape is home to a variety of birds of prey, you may see Buzzard, Hen Harriers, Peregrine Falcon and Little, Short-Eared and Barn Owls; listen out too for the distinct loud, laughing call of the Green Woodpecker.

Walk along the road from The Hey to the point where it kinks to pass through the line of the old thorn fence, a point marked by a single stone gatepost. Here, go through the field gate to the right and walk alongside the fence/ditch on your left to the end of the pasture. You now need to enter the area of woodland ahead, the easiest if not most convenient way is to climb the fence where the ditch passes beneath it. Walk ahead across the boggy patch and alongside the fence, making your way through the trees and downhill as best you can to the small gate through the fence at the bottom of the slope. Ford the stream beyond this and then scramble up the steep slope opposite, following the obvious but narrow path with a brook in a cleft to your right.

At the top of the slope keep the fence to your right and walk on across the moorland pastures, eventually ending up about half a mile later on a farm drive just beside Beatrix Farm. Turn left and walk through the farmyard with the house and barn to your right, at the far end following the left hand track gently up the hillside. In about a hundred yards, where this track passes between two thorn trees and into a field on your right, angle off to the left up the truncated track and then walk down to the barn which you'll soon be able to see. Pass to the left of the barn and head slightly left across the field to the obvious gate at the bottom. Continue to walk downhill, heading in line for the barn on the hillside opposite. Cross the stream in the area of gnarled old woodland in the valley bottom, climb the stile beyond and walk up the old track past Rough Syke Barn, then aiming for the gate you can see on the hillcrest ahead.

Climb the railway-sleeper stile to the left of this gate and walk on along the track beyond around to the left of the hilltop. On reaching the gate on your left pass through it and walk along the track, Bull Lane. At the point where this turns sharp right pause to appreciate the view ahead which stretches across the Forest of Bowland to the Three Peaks area in the Yorkshire Dales; you should be able to make out Pen-y-Ghent and Ingleborough. Remain with the track for a few yards more until it turns sharp left, at which point go through the little wooden gate in the fence ahead, aiming then across the fields to the farm nestling beneath the trees in the distance. The fields are pock-marked with small hollows. These are natural features known as shake holes, a diagnostic feature of limestone terrain. Rainwater dissolves away locally-finely jointed lime-stone causing the land surface to sag, sometimes quite considerably where small caverns underlie the surface.

Pass through the gate to the left of the barn and walk down through the farmyard of Gamble Hole Farm. At the far end bear right immediately beyond the corrugated iron barns and follow the oak tree-lined track along the right hand edge of the field. At the far end of the field leave the track to run ahead and go through the gate to the left, then walking to the diagonally opposite left hand corner of the field you are now in. Go through the gate here and step down to the road, crossing straight over this and climbing the stone step stile through the wall opposite just left of the thorn bush. Walk ahead across the field, cross the stream on the stone slab bridge and walk up through the narrow neck of the field ahead. Once through this neck bear right and walk down the narrow field towards the small barn. Leave this field near the corner to the right of the barn and continue away from the barn to the gate through the middle of the hedge ahead. At this point the tiny village of Newton comes into view down below you. Walk to the bottom left hand corner of the field you're now in, climb the stone stile into the workyard and walk down through this yard to the road at the bottom, right in the middle of Newton.

The village is little more than a cluster of old houses and cottages around a green, there's also an old Quaker Meeting House. Walk down the road signposted to Clitheroe and pass by The Parkers Arms (Whitbread) to reach the old two-arched bridge over the Hodder. Don't cross this but take the footpath on the left immediately before the bridge, walk upstream for a few yards and go through the little gate which gives access to a stone causeway alongside the water. At the end of this leave the river for a while and walk ahead with the wall on your right. Cross the slab footbridge on your right, climb the stile and turn left, then walking along with the brook on your left. Walk towards the steep, wooded hillside ahead, go through the stile at the end and then follow the path through the woods at the foot of Great Dunnow hill. At the far end go through the kissing gate and walk ahead across the field, the mansion that is Dunnow Hall coming into view on your left. Turn left along the roughly surfaced track which cuts across the field and follow this around the foot of the woodlands away from the Hall. When you reach the lodge house at the end turn right along the road to return to Slaidburn.

Beatrix and Whin Fell, Slaidburn

10. SOUTH WEST LANCASHIRE: LYDIATE

Route: Lydiate – Walsh Hall – Clieves Hills – Bangor's Green – Downholland Cross

Distance: 8.5 miles

Map: Sheet SD 20/30 Formby and Maghull

Start: The Scotch Piper, Lydiate

Access: Lydiate village is immediately north of Maghull at the junction of the A59 and A567 roads about eight miles north of Liverpool City Centre and four miles southwest of Ormskirk. The Scotch Piper is on the A567 Maghull to Southport road about a mile north of the centre of Lydiate and is on the left as you travel towards Southport.

The Scotch Piper (051 526 0503)

Centuries ago, The Scots Piper was called The Royal Oak. The reason for this is apparent in one of the pub's three public rooms where part of a massive oak tree can still be seen; the pub was constructed around the tree which was used as a main support, a not uncommon practice in pre-Tudor days. The name Scotch Piper was adopted following the Jacobite uprising of 1745; retreating from Derby in disarray a band of Bonnie Prince Charlie's surviving troops took shelter in the pub and left one of their number, a piper, to be nursed back to health there, hidden from the avenging troops of George the Second.

Little can have changed since then or, indeed, since the remarkable tenancy of the Moorcroft family commenced in the middle of the fifteenth century. From then until 1945 the pub was owned and run by a member of the family. The thatched pub predates even them, however, dating from 1320 which makes it, as is proudly proclaimed on the front wall, the oldest pub in Lancashire. Massive beams, low ceilings and stone flagged floors are complemented by simple wooden benches, solid wooden chairs and the occasional settle in the public rooms. Emulsioned walls contrast sharply with the dark beams and few paintings, photographs or artefacts decorate the walls, this very lack seems to add to the character of the place. In season an open fire blazes in the hearth in the bar area; the bar itself is a tiny servery behind which can be glimpsed the stillage where beer is served straight from the barrel into jugs or pots. The licensee, Charlie Rigby, keeps a very tasty pint of Burtonwoods Bitter and in the winter months a strong winter ale may be available; recently this has been Old Hookey from the Hook Norton brewery in Oxfordshire.

The Scotch Piper, Lydiate

All in all it's a great basic pub, recognised as such in 1986 when CAMRA awarded it the joint top award for pub preservation. Opening hours are noon to 3 pm and 5.30 pm to 11 pm.

South West Lancashire and the Lancashire Plain

The very word "plain" strikes fear into the heart of many a walker, visions of unending tracts of the flat, virtually featureless countryside of parts of East Anglia or the Netherlands haunting their dreams. The Lancashire Plain is not like that. Certainly, this area of Lancashire is characterized by drainage ditches, hedgeless fields and rich farmland intensively used by market gardeners and to this extent it resembles Holland. Where it scores its advantages, however, are in the low, wooded ridges which cut into the area, the old villages that dot the plain and the ever-present views to the looming mass of the West Pennines and the Upholland Hills immediately to the east. These features combine to offer easy, pleasant walking through ever-changing farmland and gently undulating countryside.

The rich, black soil of the area is a result of inundation by the sea following the last great ice age some ten thousand years ago; a combination of silts and sands makes this area one of the market gardens of England, famed for root crops, lettuce and brassicates. Until the 1960's trainloads of produce travelled overnight on special trains to the great London markets at Covent Garden and Nine Elms. The soils were made cultivable largely in the Eighteenth and early Nineteenth centuries by construction of drainage ditches; windmills once provided the wherewithal to pump the water into these ditches but they have now been replaced by electric pumps.

Prior to this time the area was largely low lying rough pasture and marsh, the famous Lancashire Mosslands. Powerful families such as the Asshetons and the Heskeths owned the land alongside a number of monastic foundations; income was generated from vaccaries (cattle farms) and from flax and hemp growing for the fledgling linen industry. Settlements grew up and villages developed on any available high ground – low sandy ridges and clayey knolls – as any sweeping view around the horizon will today testify; squat, sandstone church spires and towers seem to be everywhere in this once staunchly Catholic area.

The first stirrings of the Pennines mark the eastern edge of the Plain and are a convenient boundary for South West Lancashire. The ridge of the Upholland Hills reaches only very modest heights at Harrock and Billinge Hills and bears no resemblance to the "Backbone of England" just a few miles beyond, being an extension of the New Red Sandstones more familiar in Cheshire rather than the older Millstone Grits of the high Pennines.

The Walk

Leave the pub and turn right, heading south along the road towards Lydiate village centre. On reaching the bridge over the canal cross the road and take the footpath at the far end of the bridge, signposted to Pygon's Hill Lane. This brings you down to the Leeds and Liverpool

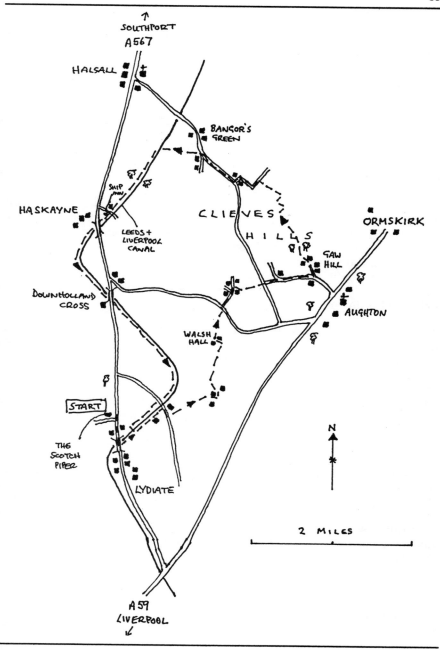

Canal on the opposite side to the tow-path. Walk along, with the water on your left, for about a mile. Many of the pastures hereabouts are in use as paddocks for racehorses, there's also a rich variety of waterbirds on and around the canal which here is thickly lined with willow trees and more akin to a natural watercourse.

Just past the cottages is a semi-circular embayment in the canal bank. This is a winding hole (pronounced as in "Wind in the Willows"), used as a place to turn boats; all canals have one every few miles. On reaching the narrow road just past this leave the canal and turn right along the road. About a hundred yards along on the right is a private drive leading to Jackson's Bridge Farm. Opposite this is a somewhat hidden public footpath sign to Back Lane. Take this path, sticking to the fence on your left. Cross the wide bridge over the drainage ditch and bear half right. The path is fairly obvious – in line of sight it heads for the church steeple on the horizon – and leads diagonally across the field to two hazel trees, the tallest remaining in a threadbare hedge. This in itself is unusual as you'll see few hedges on this walk; field boundaries are marked largely by dykes, drainage ditches or farm tracks and are often rich in wild flowers.

Keeping the hazel trees, then the ditch, on your right walk for a few hundred yards north east towards the low ridge of the Clieves Hills. At this point the right of way takes an illogical diversion. Ahead of you is a small clump of trees, to the right three sets of buildings. You should turn right when opposite the middle set and aim for the right of these cottages. On gaining the roadway here turn left and walk for about a hundred yards. Ahead on your left is a white metal fence and about twenty yards before this are two wooden posts also on the left, these mark the footpath. There is a broken down footpath sign to "Birches Brow $1/2$ mile" here at the time of writing. Head for the clump of willows and skirt these on the left, following the obvious track between the fields to reach Walsh Hall Farm. Many of the rather gnarled trees in this area display a distinctive pattern of growth on their eastward side making them seem to lean to the right. This is due to the effect of the prevailing south west wind which whips in across the plain from Liverpool Bay, half a dozen miles to the west, most branches growing on the sheltered leeward side of the trees. Pass between the barn on your right and the farmhouse off to your left, turn right along the driveway and walk along to the main road.

Turn left along the road and then almost immediately right up Clieves Hills Lane. Follow the gentle slope uphill past Firs Lane and then take the track off to the right about twenty yards before the cream-painted house on the left. The track leads up past a cottage on your right, the garden to your left boasts a resident peacock. Follow the track into the fields, home to a large number of Grey Partridge. To the right (south) are extensive views across Liverpool; you can easily pick out the two cathedrals, one at each end of Lord Street, and the cranes at the docks. Beyond is the sandstone ridge which forms the spine of the Wirral Peninsular and further still the mountains of both north east Wales and Snowdonia. You can also pick out the massive limestone headland of the Great Orme at Llandudno, named after the same Saint as the town of Ormskirk.

Aim to leave the fields to the left of the two modern houses and go straight across the road into Small Lane, bearing right at the end into Gaw Hill Lane. Remain with this, named after the highest point in the Clieves Hills at 266 feet, and climb gently up onto the ridge of the hills. Turn left along Holly Lane and walk northwards just below the ridge top. Views to the west stretch across the plain, dotted with copses, farms and myriad churchtowers, to a ridge of hills clothed in conifers. These are the Formby Hills, a series of dunes and ridges stretching up along the coast towards Southport and a National Nature Reserve famed for red squirrels and natterjack toads. Bear left with the road and then right immediately past the terrace of cottages, following this track for several hundred yards until it bends off to the right. Ahead, the large gasometer marks the position of Southport, beyond this the famous tower at Blackpool and on the far horizon the hills of the southern Lake District.

Where the track bends right you should veer left and walk to the area of scrub oak, gorse bushes, bracken and brambles. Several paths leave this area, you want the one which leads steeply downhill and directly towards the spire of Halsall church some three miles distant; the path passes an isolated oak tree and follows the line of a ditch. Skirt the clump of willows to their left and once round them turn to face a further clump of willows on your left. Walk towards these for about twenty yards then turn right and walk to yet another clump. At these turn left and follow the developing track along to the minor road. Turn left and then follow this road round the right-angled bend and along to the farm. The barn on the right has a datestone of 1802 high up on the front wall.

At the road junction at this farm turn right along Narrow Lane and walk along to the next junction, here going straight on towards the hamlet of Bangor's Green. Where the road bends sharply right look for the obvious path just to the right of the chevrons and which follows the top of a dyke bank. Walk along this path with the dyke to your left, continue straight ahead at its end and keep the resultant ditch to your right. The path brings you to a bridge over the canal; cross this, walk down the steps to the tow-path and turn right, the canal to your left. Remain now with the tow-path to return to Lydiate about three miles away. The fields here are often host to vast flocks of pink footed geese and ringed plover and patrolled by kestrel, sparrowhawk and fox. The canal winds past small villages and some large old farmhouses as well as two pubs, The Ship Inn at Haskayne (food but no real ale) and The Scarisbrick Arms Hotel at Downholland Cross (food, beer uncertain as Greenall Whitley no longer brew). Remain on the tow-path at Bridge 19, passing opposite the winding hole and cottages mentioned earlier. At the next bridge climb the steps at the far side, cross the canal and turn right, retracing the path back to the road bridge. Regain the main road here and turn right to return to the pub.

11. SOUTH WEST LANCASHIRE: CROSTON

Route: Croston – Eccleston – Heskin Old Hall – Croston Moss

Distance: 6 Miles

Map: Sheet 699 Chorley and Burscough Bridge

Start: The Lord Nelson, Croston

Access: Croston is on the A581 road about six miles west of Chorley. The Lord Nelson is at the heart of the village, facing the green to your right as you wind along the village's narrow main street. The village has a railway station on the line between Preston and Ormskirk with an hourly service on Mondays to Saturdays (no Sunday trains) and connections to Liverpool Central at Ormskirk; it is about half a mile's walk from the pub.

The Lord Nelson (0772 600387)

Named after the eponymous naval hero the pub was, prior to 1805, known as the Green Man. Its early history is uncertain but the thick, solid walls, beams and low ceilings suggest a respectable age. What is certain is that until after the second war the pub was an integral part of a village farmhouse; such dual use of a property was common in centuries past and many village ale-house first appeared as an offshoot of a farmers, potters, thatchers or smiths business.

The one bar is in the middle one of the three small rooms, each comfortably furnished and decorated with paintings and prints depicting scenes from the life and times of Horatio Nelson. A fourth room, virtually behind the bar, acts as a small restaurant. The bar sports handpumps offering Higsons and Boddingtons bitters, both excellently kept by the enthusiastic and knowledgeable landlord Jeremey Stanford-Davis who, despite his youthful years, has a long pedigree in the art of keeping and purveying real ale. Something of a pub purist, its refreshing to note that he refuses to entertain the notion of installing a jukebox or fruit machine. The main room is warmed by a roaring fire in the winter months whilst the back room has a magnificent old range manufactured by a local firm, Bamforth's of Ormskirk.

Lord Nelson, Croston

The pub overlooks its car park to the village green beyond. Emphasizing the Nelson theme, a spar above the door into the pub carries, in signal flags, the famous message "England expects..(etc)." Bar meals are available daily between noon and 2 pmand 6 pm to 9.30 pm as are meals in the restaurant; the landlord intends to further develop the range of food available but the choice is already substantial. Opening hours are noon to 3 pm and 5.30 pm to 11 pm, children are welcome.

Croston

Substantial modern developments and infilling may have considerably increased its overall population in recent years but the ancient core of the village, along the winding main street and adjoining the green, has helped it retain its character. Old brick, stone and whitewashed cottages jumbled together are backed by barns and farmyards in a compact centre where an annual market and fair has been chartered since 1283.

The river Yarrow is channelled through the village in a deep, winding, stone trough although even this does not stop periodic floods inundating the village centre. A magnificent cobbled packhorse bridge dating from 1682 spans the river towards the eastern end of the main street; the view across this to Church Street and the askew tower of St. Michael and All Angels Church is virtually unaltered since the street was last rebuilt about three hundred years ago. Originally founded in AD651 the church is typical of many in this part of Lancashire, its solid, mellow sandstone tower dominating the horizon. The churchyard also houses the village school, founded by John of Gaunt in 1372 although the contemporary building is somewhat younger.

The village lies towards the edge of the Lancashire Plain, bordered to the south by the low lying Croston Moss, drained in the late Eighteenth Century to provide rich farmland. To the east the land rises slowly to the high West Pennines, source of the Yarrow which joins the River Douglas immediately west of Croston and thence flows to the Ribble Estuary some eight miles west of Preston. Little evidence remains of the pre-war industries which once made the village self sufficient; cotton mills, brickworks, feed mills and the gasworks have all vanished, only one animal feedstuffs mill survives to the east of the village. Mirroring this change the number of pubs has been halved in the same period.

The Walk

Walk to the main road at the far end of the green from the pub and turn left along the main street. At the point where this bears sharp left continue straight ahead past the old cross and along Church Street, entering the churchyard at the far end. Pass between the tower and the school and leave the churchyard at the green posts, following the river, to your right, upstream. Leave the meadow via the stile beside the low, white cottage and turn right along the minor road, Grape Lane, remaining with this until you reach a bridge across the Yarrow about half a mile distant. Don't cross this bridge but bear left just beforehand at the public footpath sign for Highfield Road and Eccleston, presently crossing a stile and thereafter remaining with the riverbank. The small weir marks the start of the mill leat which once fed water to Croston Mill, still in operation on the far riverbank but no longer dependent on the river. Beside the weir is a small concrete shed with an aerial, this appears to be an automatic river gauge, feeding information to the local water company via radio waves, the power for the transmitter coming from a solar panel on the shed roof.

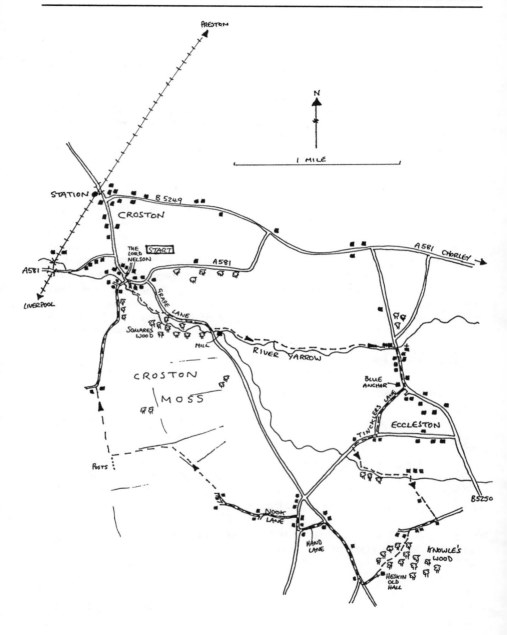

Remain with the river for the next mile or so; the path is well used and leads to the village of Eccleston. Walk in front of the cottages to the road and turn right, crossing the bridge and entering the edge of the village. Pass the Blue Anchor pub on your right and then turn right along Tincklers Lane. This skirts the north western edge of Eccleston and is somewhat windy and busy so care is counselled. At the T-junction turn right along the road which retains the name Tincklers Lane and remain with it for several hundred yards. Once past Tincklers Lane Cottage on your right cross to the left of the road and keep your eyes peeled for a stile well hidden in behind the line of the hedge. Cross this and follow the line of the hedge beyond virtually down to the stream, immediately before reaching which you should cross a stile on your left and, from here, follow the stream upstream for nearly half a mile.

On reaching the housing estate look for the footbridge across the stream – half right across the meadow – and cross this, then the stile immediately beyond. Walk straight up the field ahead of you and then into the next field via any of the wide gaps in the old hedge. Here, head half left and aim for the sheds and white cottage at the end of this field. Leave the field by the stile next to the farmyard gate and then follow the drive away from the cottage, Shelbourne House Farm, to the narrow road at the end, turning right along this which soon deteriorates into a farm track. Pass two bungalows on your left and then take the footpath on the left, signposted to Halfpenny Lane. Keep to the left of the wooden sheds and enter the field at the end via the stile, walk ahead to the woods at the end and enter them over a further stile.

A roughly cobbled track leads down to a wooden footbridge across the stream at the bottom of this peaceful wooded dingle. Cross the bridge and follow the track ahead up the far side of the steep valley, remaining within the narrow band of trees until the path eventually emerges into the driveway of Heskin Old Hall, the solid stone farm to your left. Walk ahead along the drive to the minor road and turn right, then right again at the triangular green into Tannersmith Lane. Continue along here for about a third of a mile and turn left along Hand Lane – it's the first left turn you reach. At the far end turn right and walk for about a hundred yards until you reach Robin Hood Cottage on your right, the stone plaque high on the wall dating it to 1889. Opposite this is Nook Lane along which you should wind for the next mile or so, following the footpath sign where appropriate towards Meadow Lane.

The road goes imperceptibly downhill, leaving the low, undulating countryside behind and leading down to Croston Moss. Bear right at the

Pack Horse Bridge, Croston

fork to walk between the farm on your left and the barns on your right; then where the track turns away to the left carry straight ahead, joining the line of a hedge on your left. Where the hedge peters out bear slightly left and walk along the line of the track, remaining with this for about a third of a mile and passing between fields of vegetables. The mossland is dotted with spinneys; ahead a long low ridge marks the site of Rufford village and the line of the railway. Pass by a ditch which comes in at a right angle from your right. Several hundred yards further on another ditch comes in at an acute angle from the right, at this point you should bear left and follow the ditch to a line of four wooden posts about two hundred yards away.

Pause here to appreciate the views behind across the gentle countryside you've walked through to the distinct profile of Winter Hill, topped by transmitters, at the heart of the West Pennine Moors; to your left is nearby Harrock Hill and, virtually in line with the wooden posts, the obelisk on top of Ashurst's Beacon. From these poles turn right along the track and walk towards the farm and barns some distance away. Bear right as you reach the farm then almost immediately left and follow the by-now surfaced lane back to Croston. Turn right at the end, cross the packhorse bridge and then turn left to reach the green and The Lord Nelson.

12. SOUTH WEST LANCASHIRE: DALTON

Route: Walthew Park – Dean Wood – Gathurst – Leeds & Liverpool Canal – Appley Bridge – Ashurst's Beacon

Distance: 7.5 Miles

Map: Sheet SD 40/50 Wigan and Ormskirk

Start: The Prince William Inn, Dalton

Access: The pub is very close to Ashurst's Beacon, a prominent landmark some five miles west of Wigan. From Wigan take the A577 through Orrell towards Skelmersdale, passing very close to Junction 26 on the M6. Go round the tight hairpin bend in Upholland and continue for about 400 yards to the Victoria Hotel on the right. The minor road immediately before this on the right, Mill Lane, leads along to the Prince William which is about half a mile past the Country Park and on the right.

By rail you can pick up the walk at either Gathurst or Appley Bridge stations, both of which are on the regular, daily, Manchester to Southport (via Wigan Wallgate) service.

The Prince William (0695 623989)

Ramblers with a Royalist bent will particularly appreciate this long established pub in a dominant position close to the summit of Ashurst's Beacon. In recent years it has seen an extension and extensive redecoration but retains its weather-beaten old sign depicting Prince William, later the fourth King George who lived from 1765-1837. The open-plan pub is comfortably furnished and internal wall decorations reflect its name; there are family trees of the royal family since medieval times and paintings, photographs and momentos of significant royal events in the past. The beer comes from Burtonwoods brewery near Warrington, both the Best Bitter and the Dark Mild being available from a range of handpumps along the long bar which serves the one large room the pub offers. An adjoining room has been converted into an a la carte restaurant.

Complementing the draught Burtonwoods is a daily selection of bar snacks and meals, invariably offering a vegetarian option; food is available from noon to 2 pm and 7 pm to 10 pm (approximately). The pub itself is open all day every day (standard hours on Sundays) and is a popular meeting place for rambling groups on this high ridge above industrial Lancashire. Children are actively encouraged – there's even a crazy golf course in the pub's beer garden.

Ashurst's Beacon

About three hundred yards north of the pub and just behind the neighbouring Beacon Inn, Ashurst's Beacon is the highest point in the line of low hills which mark the end of the Lancashire Plain to the west and the first rumblings of the Pennines to the east. Both these features are easily visible from the top on a clear day from what is one of the best viewpoints in Lancashire; virtually the whole of the County is visible and those with binoculars should be able to discern up to four National Parks – The Lake District, Snowdonia, The Yorkshire Dales and The Peak District.

At around 580 feet above sea level, it is crowned by a monument which is a cross between a tower and an obelisk. This was constructed in 1798 as one of a series of beacon towers built throughout the length and breadth of England at a time when invasion by Napoleon seemed a certainty, they were to act as early warnings of such an invasion. There is little doubt that similar use was made of this lofty perch over two centuries earlier when beacons were prepared to warn of the Spanish Armada in 1588. A short distance to the north-west of the hilltop is Ashurst's Hall, home to the family after which the hill is named; the poet Byron had connections with the family but whether he stayed in the area is unrecorded. The Beacon is part of Beacon Country Park, developed to benefit the residents of nearby Skelmersdale, a new town on the Plain immediately west of the Park. Facilities include a visitor centre, nature trails and a golf course and driving range; these are off the ridge-top road about half a mile south of the Prince William.

The Walk

Leave the car park of the Prince William and turn right along Beacon Lane. Almost immediately turn right again into Long Heys Lane and

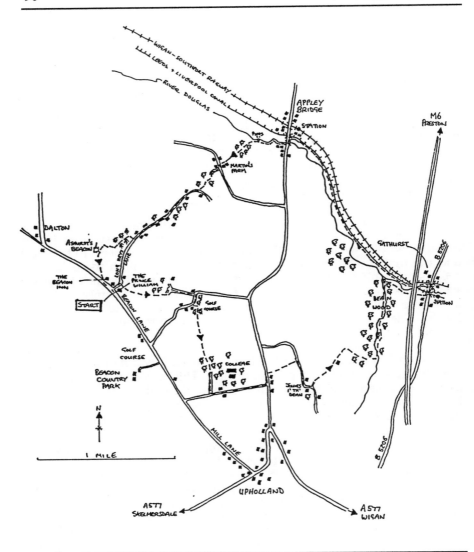

walk along this for about a hundred yards. At this point you reach on
your right the entrance to a rail-fenced car park, there's also a yellow
waymark arrow nailed to a tree. Turn right here and stick to the right
hand edge, a rutted track developing almost immediately. Follow this
track around, the car park petering out on the left whilst to the right is

the village cricket pitch. As the track fails continue straight ahead, sticking to the hedge on your left. At the gap, virtually opposite the thin wedge of trees, change to the other side of the hedge and walk downhill, keeping close to the hedge. At the bottom, join the rough road and turn left.

Visible some distance ahead of you is a fine old building, Stone Hall. You, however, should turn right at the triangular junction marked by a large ash tree and walk down along this rough road for about a quarter of a mile to the point where it issues onto a minor road in front of a red-roofed bungalow. Turn right here and walk along the straight. At the end of this straight, and immediately before the garage, a stile on the left, marked by a yellow hydrant plate, leads onto a small golf course. Climb this stile and walk directly forwards across the fairway, aiming for the tall ash tree in the woods beyond (as a further guide there are seven smaller trees growing in a line about five yards out from the far edge of the fairway, you need to pass to the right of the farthest-left tree). Walk virtually straight through the woods here, slightly favouring your right hand. At the far side a large field opens out. You should remain just in the woods and turn right, following the indistinct path until it, too, leaves the woods at a point marked by a boulder.

The way now is straight on, keeping the hedge to your left until a rough track is gained, lined on the right by an infilled quarry. Walk along this track, rich in wildflowers from spring to late autumn, bearing left where necessary as you walk through the oak and beech woodlands. At the T-junction at the end of the track turn left and walk downhill through the area of farm buildings to join a surfaced road, passing a red brick house on your right. Hidden in the trees on the left is the substantial St. Josephs College in Walthew Park, once a seminary for training Catholic priests but now a College of Theology.

At the bottom turn left along the main road, cross it and about twenty yards beyond the last bungalow turn right into the field, following the line of telegraph poles down the gentle slope. There's a small stone quarry being worked on your right so don't be alarmed to hear explosions from time to time. Forming the horizon ahead is a long, low line of hills to the north of Wigan, part of the large Haigh Country Park; nearer to hand is the M6 Motorway and the massive H.J. Heinz factory. On reaching the minor road turn right and follow it for about a third of a mile, bearing sharp left and going downhill to a sharp right hand bend at Jollies i'th' Dean Farm. At this spot is a small duckpond populated by a wide variety of duck and geese, some wooden huts in the trees and an immense number of "domestic" rabbits hopping about the area.

Here turn left up the drive dedicated to Dean Wood Farm. Follow the track past several stables and stock-rearing sheds on your right to the point where the fence ends and a public footpath sign points right. Take this path, remaining outside the wire and follow the obvious path down into the trees just as the woods close in at the corner of the field. A steep scramble down over natural sandstone steps and ledges brings you to the stream which flows through these quiet, peaceful woodlands, Dean Woods. Shortly you'll come to two footbridges, one metal, one wooden. Cross the metal one and bear left uphill at the far side, following the path up through the woods. Bear right at the fork to emerge at the woodland edge beside a barbed wire fence. To you right is a stile, cross this and turn left to follow the woodland edge.

Passing through a further stile on your left, continue forward but this time on the woodland side of the fence, working gradually down into the woods to pick up a more obvious track running high above the deepening valley. Walk right down this path, crossing fallen trees and passing massive bracket fungi adorning dead tree stumps. You reach the stream at some rough stepping stones, decidedly slippery and undoubtedly underwater after prolonged heavy rain. Cross the stream here, which marks the Lancashire/Greater Manchester boundary, and continue downstream, keeping the main watercourse to your right, fording a further two side streams before crossing the green footbridge that appears on your right. Follow the track away left from this and emerge from the woodland on the valley floor of the River Douglas.

Ahead, the massive viaduct that carries the M6 seventy feet above the river dominates the view, to the left the Leeds and Liverpool Canal and the Wigan to Southport railway follow the river through this deep, winding section of valley. Remain with the track, pass beneath the viaduct and walk to the end to join the B5206 road near Gathurst station. Turn left, pass under the railway and cross the river bridge, then look for the blue cycleway sign pointing left towards Burscough; following the direction of this sign takes you down to the canal tow-path not far from the Navigation Pub (Tetleys beers, bar food).

For the next mile and a half stick with the tow-path, the canal to your right. There's an impressive view of the M6 crossing high over the railway line which in turn passes low over the canal, the river just off to the left. Beyond this the lock keepers cottage at Dean Locks is passed by on a long, cobbled section of tow-path, just remain to the left of the canal and wind round the back of the cottage. A very scenic part of the walk now follows, the sound of the M6 dying off and the canal winding along the contour about twenty feet above the river, all well wooded and with views ahead to Parbold Hill. Pause at the second swingbridge you come to and look directly left to see the obelisk atop Ashurst's Beacon, your destination still several miles distant.

Ashurst's Beacon

On reaching Appley Bridge leave the tow-path and turn left down the road, almost immediately crossing the river bridge. Straightaway look on the right for a narrow path threading along between the cottages and the river and walk along this, cottage gardens and allotments to your left. Stay with the riverbank until you've passed the collection of large pipes which cross and/or stand upright by the river. A short, broken section of fencing is immediately ahead of you whilst to your left, beyond some concrete slabs, is a truncated hedge. Walk across the field to this hedge and then follow its line, keeping it to your left. Where it finishes walk straight forward to the brook and narrow strip of woodland. There is a crossing just to your right, marked by a piece of green card attached to a tree. Cross the brook here then turn left, following the obvious path as it winds up through the woodland. Emerging from these woods a large renovated house and quasi-detached garage are on your left; the definitive right of way skirts the very edge of the garden straight ahead to emerge onto a narrow road next to the small electricity transformer, located as Martins Farm.

Turn left along this road and then take the rough lane on the right just past the cottages, following this as it winds gently uphill. At the point where it splits three ways you should take the narrow middle option, cutting through the bank and again marked by a piece of green card. Follow the path along to a stream, cross this and then walk up the far bank, the path here and there using natural rock steps to gain height. On reaching the minor road turn right and follow it uphill, ignoring the track that almost immediately branches off to the right.

After about half a mile pass by the renovated Catteralls Farm and barn off to your left. Wind round the bends above this and keep your eyes peeled for a gap in the high bank to your right – it's directly opposite where the spinney on your left peters out to a point. Go up through this gap and climb to the field. Stick with the right hand edge and follow it round until you see a footbridge down in the deep wooded clough on your right. Cross this, and the stile beyond, and turn left, walking up the left hand edge of the field to a further stile near the top beside a five-barred gate. Cross this and walk on into the woodland, then after about two hundred yards take any one of the tracks on your right up through the trees to reach the monument on top of Ashurst's Beacon. Ahead of you, far below, is Skelmersdale. Walk along the ridge with the town down to your right, cross the stile and follow the track down along to the minor road. Turn left up this, pass the Beacon Inn and return to the Prince William about two hundred yards further on.

13. THE FYLDE: WHARLES

Route: Wharles – Medlar – Scholar Bridge – Elswick – Crossmoor

Distance: 7 Miles

Map: Sheet SD 43/53 Preston (North) and Kirkham (Lancs)

Start: The Eagle and Child, Wharles

Access: From Blackpool take the A586 road towards Garstang, Lancaster and M6 (North). Turn right at the major junction east of Little Singleton and go south along the A585 towards Kirkham, the M55, Preston and M6(South). After about a mile turn left along the B5269 towards Longridge. Turn first left and on reaching Elswick wind through the village and turn right at the far end down the minor road to Roseacre (the turn is by the corner shop and before the church). Follow this road to its end at the T-junction and turn right to reach the pub. From Preston take the A583 then the A585 to Kirkham. Look for the turn to the right just after the old windmill as you enter Kirkham, turning along here will bring you to the pub in about 2.5 miles.

The Eagle and Child (0772 690312)

(Please note that the Eagle and Child is only open from 7 pm to 11 pm on Mondays to Fridays; at weekends the pub is open from noon to 3 pm in addition to these evening hours. Alternative pubs are available in Elswick for midweek walkers, these are outlined below.)

The Fylde retains a significant number of country inns hidden "in the middle of nowhere" down endlessly winding country lanes. The Eagle and Child is one of the best of these, an isolated, thatched cottage which originated as a farmhouse in the 1600's. The name comes from the family crest of the Earls of Derby who once owned much of the Fylde area. Much of its early trade must have come from the agricultural community which farmed the rich local land, supplemented later by workers at the now closed brickworks in Wharles hamlet. Nowadays the majority of trade comes by car from Blackpool, Preston and across the south Fylde area.

They come for the beer, the reputation of which ensures busy evening trade for the landlord Mr. Tatham. As the large collection of pump clips behind the bar testifies, he ensures an ever changing array of ales from throughout England and Wales, usually supplied direct from the brewery rather than from a wholesaler. On offer on my last visit were Marstons Pedigree, Wadworths 6X (Wiltshire), Hardy Hanson's Kimberley Ale (Nottingham) and Boddingtons Bitter, all hand pumped. Other beers were already settling in the cellar for later in the week, emphasizing the popularity of the pub in spite of its limited weekday hours.

To drink the beers in, there is one large room furnished with a wide variety of tables and seating including some beautiful intricately carved benches and settles in the alcove beyond the bar. The pub has two real fires, the one on the right as you go in has a magnificently carved wooden mantle and surround, next to which on the wall is the largest brass plate you're ever likely to see. Dotted here and there are long-case clocks and hanging from the beams the tools of bygone smiths and carpenters trades. The pub doesn't offer any food despite the entry in the "Good Food Guide" which has the landlord totally perplexed.

Eagle and Child, Wharles

The alternative pubs to use if you wish to enjoy this walk on a weekday lunchtime are both in Elswick. The Ship Hotel is a recently refurbished Boddingtons pub with a large garden; The Boot and Shoe is a fairly modern Thwaites pub, both pubs offer bar meals. Directions to both of these are included in the walk.

THE FYLDE

Picture an area which was scraped flat and clean by glaciers ten thousand years ago. When the ice retreated it left mounds and ridges of sands and gravels standing out from a plain covered with boulder clay and dank marshes, the whole rarely more than a few feet above sea level and well wooded. This is the landscape the Romans found when they claimed the area two thousand years ago. They built a port at the now lost Portus Stetenorium (assumed to be somewhere near present day Kirkham and a victim of the shifting coastline in this area, no positive remains have been found) but did little to change the surrounding countryside. The original native settlers gave us the name of the area. Fylde is derived from the Old English "gefilde" meaning, simply, "plain," and includes the coastline, salt marshes, estuaries and low lands between the Lune in the north and the Ribble in the south.

Only in the late eighteenth and nineteenth centuries did the Fylde we know today come into being. The neat areas of woodland, spinneys and copses that break up the landscape, the isolated farmsteads nestling on almost every slight hummock or ridge in the area and the compact local villages are largely a product of the era of the land drainers. These were a breed of engineers and visionaries who used wind power to help drain the vast areas of marsh, mossland and thick clayey soils, creating a complex network of drainage channels and resulting in very rich farmland underlain by hundreds of miles of clay field drains. There was even a patron saint of underdrainers, St. Eloi. Only a handful of the hundreds of windmills that once characterised the Fylde now remain, none used for their original purpose.

The Fylde is probably best known today for the holiday resorts at Blackpool and Lytham – St. Annes, none of which was more than a few fishermens huts until well into the Victorian era, and for Fleetwood, essentially a failed railway company resort town which developed into one of the top fishing ports in Britain before recession virtually destroyed this industry. If these rather brash places are your idea of the Fylde then put aside this prejudice for a day or two and try the suggested walks which are guaranteed to offer you a fresh perspective on Blackpool's back door; undemanding, peaceful and packed with interest for nature lovers.

The Walk

(The green lane beyond Medlar Hall may have deep mud after heavy rain).

Walk along the road directly opposite the pub, Moorside, following the sign for Kirkham. Go round the bend and start to climb slowly uphill. About a hundred yards before the top of the rise are two field gates on opposite sides of the road. You should go through the one on the right. bear right to the hedge and follow the line of this away from the road for the length of two fields. At the end of the second field you'll find some gates at the end of a lane. Go through the gate out of the field and then cross the stile beside the gate ahead of you, turning left and following the line of the hedge. Pass the end of the woodland and carry on along with the line of the fence. From the point where this turns right walk straight ahead across the field heading towards the farm you can see in the distance (n.b. not the farm off to your left), South Greenhills.

On this line of sight continue across a series of stiles to reach a footbridge over a drainage ditch. Cross this, turn right and walk to the hedge, whereupon turn left and follow its line up across two fields. Go through the gate at the end and then through the gate immediately on your left (do not go down the farm track). Turn right and follow the field boundary down along in front of the farm's garden. Cross the stile at the end and turn right up to the surfaced road, then turn left along this. Remain with this as it winds around and bends sharp right past the farm called Leyland Hall. Off to the left is a low marshy area with a number of ponds teeming with wildfowl; this walk passes a large number of such areas, some are natural, some marl holes dug by farmers in the past. At the next sharp left turn, marked by a copse of trees around a pond, go straight on and down the green lane ahead; to the right is Medlar Hall Farm. Pass through a gate across the track and follow this winding, sometimes very muddy, track right to its end where it peters out completely at the corner of a field by an old wooden shack.

From the corner near the shack walk along the edge of the field following the right hand boundary, pass through an old field gate and walk ahead to a footbridge across a field drain. Do not cross this bridge but instead turn left and follow the line of the drain along the edge of the pasture. At the end of the field cross the substantial concrete-slab

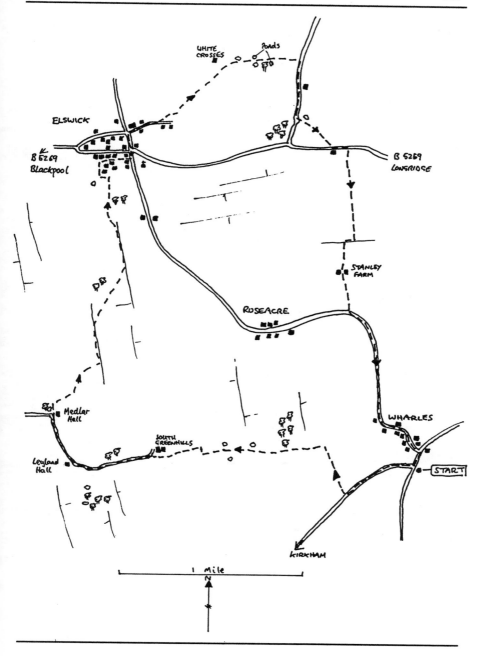

footbridge, known locally as Scholar Bridge, and then bear half right across the narrow field to join the line of another drain, then following this up the edge of this long field. Pass a stand of trees on your left and continue on to the far end of the field. At the rough hedge here turn left and walk to the corner of the field to the stile marked by a boulder. Climb over the stile and then keep the hedge to your right , walking up to a narrow gap stile beside a field gate and then along the edge of another long field, passing the end of a farm track as you do so.

Once past this track look ahead to the far boundary hedge and aim to meet this roughly half way across, in line with the gabled terraced houses in the distance. Cross the footbridge at this point and walk ahead to the end of the field. On reaching the fenced gardens turn left to gain a stile at the corner. Cross this, turn right and walk to the stile out of this field, once across which turn right along the footpath that winds up between the houses (i.e. not the one along the roadside).

Go straight past the group of swings and a slide (a path, left, from here leads directly to The Ship Hotel) and remain with the path as it passes through this modern estate in Elswick village. Go straight over the estate road and continue ahead, shortly passing a hauliers yard on your left. At the end turn left and walk to the crossroads. Go straight across and walk to Bonds Ice Cream Parlour at the far end, here turning right along Bonds Lane (if you look left at this point you'll see the Boot and Shoe pub). Walk along for some distance to reach, on your right, a sign-board for some kennels. On your left at this juncture your route is signalled by a public footpath sign. Follow the well trodden path across the field, cross the stile and walk ahead to the next stile just beyond the black drain cover. Once over this aim for the far left corner of the field and negotiate the rickety stile here, then walk virtually straight ahead, keeping to the left of the field and heading towards the isolated cottage.

Ignore the stile on your left which would take you to this cottage and walk on to the end of the field, crossing the small bridge here. Aim now towards the right hand clump of scrubby trees ahead of you, passing en route on your left a pond surrounded by trees and bushes. You should arrive at a stile over a fence on a narrow neck of land between two further ponds. Cross the stile and bear right following the fence along past the spinney and, eventually, to a minor road. Turn right along this road.

Pass the farm and stick with the road until the obvious kink. Here, take the stile beneath the two trees on your left and aim for the farm across the field, leaving via the white gate at the far side. Turn left along the road here and walk for about a hundred yards to the point where the road bends to the right. At this point look on the right for a well hidden stile, cross this and walk with the line of fence across the paddock. Cross the stile at the far side and walk to the offset corner of the field not far ahead. Here cross the stile into the large field and keep the consequent line of hedge on your right for a further three fields to reach a footbridge. Cross this and turn right to follow the ditch for about a hundred yards, then look directly left across the field to a farm gate. Walk across to this and pass through it (the right of way which lies some way to the left of this gate is blocked by a hedge, local practice seems to be to use this gate as an alternative) and then follow the track beyond to the farmyard. Go straight through the yard and along the drive at the far side, following this to the minor road at the end. Turn left along the road here, walk the remaining mile to Wharles and turn right at the junction to return to the Eagle and Child.

14. THE FYLDE: GLASSON

Route: Conder Green – Glasson – Crook Farm – Cockersand Abbey – Hillam – Thurnham

Distance: 7.5 Miles

Map: Sheet SD 45/55 Galgate and Dolphinholme

Start: The Stork Inn, Conder Green

Access: The hamlet of Conder Green is about four miles south of Lancaster on the A588 road to Cockerham and Blackpool, The Stork Inn adjoins the main road. Alternatively a minor road from the crossroads in the centre of Galgate – on the A6 and just north of junction 33 on the M6 – is signposted to Conder Green (turn off the A6 by the Green Dragon and bear left just after the viaduct). The Stork is at the end of this minor road where it joins the A588.

The Stork Inn (0524 751234)

This is a great pub to be at on a cold, almost still, winters morning when the marshes are at their best, wraith-like mists rising from the channels which thread the area, the eerie echoes and calls of unseen flights of wading birds and the gaunt ribs of rotting boats rising from the mudbanks, ephemeral in the drifting fog.

A pub has stood at the edge of the sea marsh here for at least 330 years; mention of it was made in a document recording local celebrations to mark the restoration to the throne of Charles 2 in 1660. In those days it was known as The Cocks, believed to reflect strong local interest in the then-popular pastime of cock fighting. By 1807 the long, low, oak panelled pub was named Duke Hamilton's Arms after the local Lord of the Manor. One of the Hamilton family houses was Ashton Hall, a mile to the north of the pub. The same Hamilton family had as a member a certain Emma, Lady Hamilton. It is said that Nelson once moored off Glasson and hired a renowned local river pilot, a blind man, to help him reach the said Lady at Ashton Hall via the treacherous channels through the marshes at the dead of night. The Hall still exists as the centre-piece of a swish golf course and country club.

Stork Inn, Conder Green

The name The Stork comes from such a bird which is included in the crest of the Starkie family of Padiham who purchased the Ashton Estate in the Nineteenth century. You won't see storks on the marshes that front the pub but you may well see Swans, Shellduck, Pink Footed and Canada Geese and a wide variety of wading birds. Other regular visitors include Gypsies who stop on pastures near The Stork en route to and from the famous Appleby Horse Fair early each June; the colourful horse-drawn caravans and impromptu entertainments are a big attraction.

The year-round attraction at the pub is, however, the range of beers – electric pumped Theakstons Best, Boddingtons and Tetleys Bitters and Higsons Mild all served in comfortable surroundings – the brass and copper festooned snug has a great roaring fire in winter – by landlord Joe Davis and his extremely friendly staff. A range of bar snacks is available (look for the specials written on the blackboard) and there's a special children's menu.

Outside the pub has a well appointed play area for children; more adult pastimes will soon be complemented by a brand new Crown bowling green being laid for the pub. One hopes this won't suffer from salt pollution as the pub is occasionally completed isolated for several hours each side of high tide at the spring and autumn neaps and by occasional storm tides. Pub hours, tides allowing, are 11.30 pm to 3 pm and 6.30 pm to 11 pm (food daily noon to 2 pm, 7 pm to 9 pm in summer, Friday and Saturday evenings only in winter).

Glasson

Echoes of times past hang heavy in the air at this windswept, estuarine village which still, surprisingly, thrives in an age which has seen most similar places all-but die. Glasson's dock was developed to serve nearby Lancaster, itself a port used by seagoing vessels but prone to silting and reached only by a treacherous approach channel. The dock is at the end of a short branch of the Lancaster Canal which opened in 1799, eventually linking Preston with Kendal. The Glasson Dock branch opened in 1826 and connected the already existing dock to the canal network ensuring a rapid escalation in its fortunes at the expense of Sunderland (see North Lune section) which became a ghost port; Lancaster Port (including Glasson) was ranked as the fourth busiest British port during the first half of the nineteenth century.

The coming of the railway marked the start of a slow decline of Glasson as a port. Although linked by rail to Lancaster in 1883, earlier rail lines to Fleetwood and to Heysham, both rapidly developing harbours only a few miles from Glasson, had started to milk trade away, both passenger and freight vessels preferring the facilities at these other ports. Glasson, however, refused to die and developed a modest shipbuilding and dry dock facility whilst continuing to receive coastal traders. This resilience helped Glasson survive the withdrawal of its passenger rail service as long ago as 1930 (the line was completely closed by the Beeching axe); in the last fifteen years it has developed as a marina both for sea-going yachts and cruisers and canal craft. The dock itself remains in operation with regular shipments of timber from Scandinavia and some container and coaster work. It has also acted as a half way house for old packet steamers; the Victoria Hotel has more than a few times been dwarfed by old passenger ferries on their final journey to the breakers yard.

Cockersand Abbey

Hugh Garth was something of a local celebrity in his day. In the time of the early Normans he was treated as a saintly recluse, admired for his prowess at healing and benevolence to those in need. He lived in a hut overlooking the sands and rock ledges and became known as Hugh the

Hermit. His interests and skills were developed by his successors at the site who had established a refuge for lepers and a sanatorium for monks by the year 1200. This later grew into Cockersand Abbey, one of the major Lancashire Houses and leading seminary of the Premonstratensian (White Canons) persuasion, famed for their medical training. That its fame spread far and wide is undoubted, records exist of a pier/jetty being built to cater for trade, passengers and pilgrims travelling to/from Ireland. A lighthouse was constructed, one of the earliest in these Islands. The Reformation, however, put paid to the Abbey; many of its stones were used in marshland farms and now only the small, weather-beaten Chapter-house and a few piles of stone remain on this windswept foreshore. The Chapter-house has, in the past, seen use as a mausoleum by the Dalton family of Thurnham and is thus kept locked.

The Walk

From the Inn's door turn right along the narrow road and follow it to the car park and picnic site at the former Conder Green railway station. From here turn left to follow the old trackbed curving south on its embankment, well above the salt marshes and intricate meandering channels of the tiny River Conder as it meets the Lune estuary. Follow the old railway through to Glasson, leaving it near the Victoria Hotel (Mitchells Ales and one of three pubs around the harbour edge which all serve real ale) and cross the swing bridge across the canal between the bustling marina and the Dock itself.

Walk uphill with the road, Tithebarn Hill, to the top and bear left. This is an excellent spot to stop and take in the views; at all of 65 feet high it is one of the highest points in the whole of the Fylde. Ahead across the Lune is the lonely Sunderland Peninsular, behind you the heights of Bowland brood darkly beyond the modernist white architecture (it is supposed to mirror an Italian hill village) of Lancaster University. At your feet Glasson, further afield manmade features such as Blackpool Tower, Heysham nuclear power station and the gas platforms in Morecambe Bay. To your right, on a clear day, the mountains of the Lake District seem near enough to touch.

Descend the hill to the sharp left hand bend and here take the right-hand-most track, Marsh Lane, which wends its way past a caravan park and down onto the boggy levels of Glasson Marsh. Simply remain with the line of track across the muddy fields to reach Crook Farm, pass through the gate to the left of the buildings here and turn left along the sea wall. This is an excellent place to walk following a winters storm,

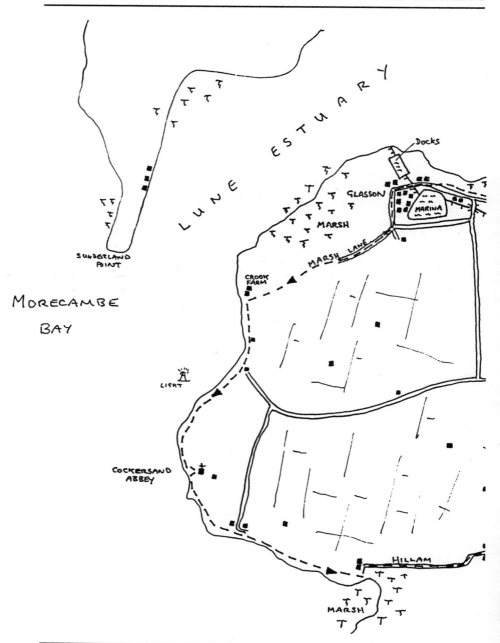

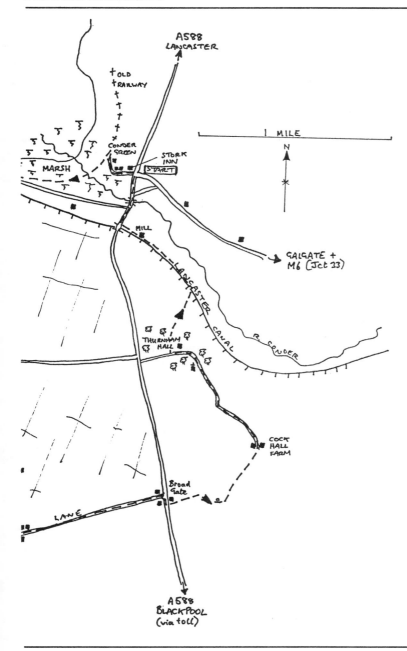

beachcombing the rocky, pebbly foreshore can produce all sorts of surprises.

Continue south along the seashore, passing by the old lookout tower and Abbey Lighthouse Cottage; the derivation of the name is obvious but the pylon has seen better days. Out across the mudflats Plover Scar Light, at the seaward edge of a shelf of sandstone, marks the start of the channel to Glasson Dock and Lancaster. At low water the flats are often busy with carts, tractors and a variety of other vehicles driven there by local shellfish gatherers who are harvesting the local cockle and mussel beds. Be wary of gathering your own, however – take note of the local warning signs. Instead leave the collecting to the regulars and to the abundance of seabirds which prompted the designation of the whole area as a wildfowl refuge back in 1963.

In a short while a minor diversion from the coastal path allows you to reach the scant remains of Cockersand Abbey. Return to the coast and continue along the path, turning east to pass by Bank Houses and a caravan park on your left. Pass the next group of buildings, Bank End Farm, and join the narrow Hillam Lane, skirting the edge of the marsh and following it over a low ridge to reach the A588 road.

Turn right, then almost immediately look for the track just beyond "Broad Gate" farm on your left – go through the middle one of three gates by the tumbledown shed. Go along the track from here and cross the stile at the end. Walk up along the greenway between the trees, then following the hedge on your right. When you reach the field gate between two stone posts pass through it and walk virtually straight ahead to reach the high point of the field, marked by trees. There's a duckpond at the top here; pass this to your left and look for the simple stile over the fence ahead just beyond the tall oak tree. Cross this and turn left downhill to reach two gates. Go through the right hand one of these, walk through this small corral and on to the end of the track by an octagonal concrete water trough. Go through the gate here and head slightly left, aiming for the concentration of farm buildings visible ahead at Cock Hill Farm. Cross the intervening hedge and stream via the footbridge and aim for the gate near the two small silo's visible in the farmyard. Enter the yard via the gate here and bear left around the barn supporting these silo's, passing by a larger barn on your left. Walk straight ahead through the yard and leave the complex past a very large barn on your right (this isn't strictly the definitive right of way but the one recommended by the Lady of the farm).

You are now on a long farm drive, wind along with it for the next mile or so. On the left you'll pass the church of St. Thomas and Elizabeth which serves the scattered community of this, Thurnham; a fine mausoleum adjoins the church tower. Continue along the drive until you reach Thurnham Hall on your right. This is the ancestral home of the Dalton family, parts of it date back to the thirteenth century. Until recently you could visit the Hall and chapel but work is currently in hand to develop a "Country Club and International Multi-Ownership Resort" (i.e. timeshare) so future access is unlikely.

Turn right to walk down along the track in front of the Hall and continue to the area of old barns on your right. Bear right past the back of these and, where the new rough road bears sharp right, turn left and walk to the old ruined barn. From here follow the sunken, tree lined greenway for a number of yards to reach a stile beside a green gate. Climb the stile and bear half-right to reach a bridge across the Glasson Dock branch of the Lancaster Canal. Walk across this and look carefully on your left before you leave the bridge to find the gap stile giving access to the tow-path. Walk along the tow-path, water to your left, passing some of the locks and reaching Thurnham Mill, an old corn mill whose long-gone machinery was once powered by water from the canal. Continue on to the road bridge and leave the tow-path here, heading north back to the Stork which is visible in the distance.

15. THE FYLDE: CUDDY HILL

Route: Cuddy Hill – Lancaster Canal – Woodplumpton – Bell Fold

Distance: 5 Miles

Map: Sheet SD 43/53 Preston (North) and Kirkham (Lancs)

Start: The Plough at Eaves, Cuddy Hill, Preston

Access: This is reputedly the most difficult pub in Lancashire to find, so if you have difficulty the Grid Reference is SD 494375. Take the A6 north from Preston to the traffic lights at Broughton and here turn left along the B5269 towards Elswick. Wind along with this for a little over a mile and turn right at the junction, remaining with the B5269. At the end of the short straight turn right along the minor road signposted to Eaves and Barton. Cross the canal and, at the junction, turn left towards Eaves. Simply keep left to arrive at the pub about a mile along on your right.

The Plough at Eaves (0772 690233)

The pub appears to be named after a local farm, the actual postal address of Cuddy Hill refers to a wide area of scattered cottages and farms here some five miles northwest of Preston. The Plough dates back as a pub to 1625, obviously a period when the average stature was somewhat more restricted than today – anyone much over six feet tall will have difficulty straightening up inside this low, heavily beamed building. It stands on the site of the Battle of Cuddy Hill which was fought in 1546, one of many skirmishes in the long-drawn out conflict between the Tudors and the Scots. A century later the pub was used as a refuge by both Royalist and Parliamentarian troops at the time of the Battle of Preston; can't you just picture the landlord forever turning around a double-sided picture of Cromwell and Charles 1, depending on which way the tide of battle was flowing?

Sadly, no such picture survives. There are, however, a lot of old prints depicting the Civil War era which the current landlord, David Atherton, unearthed during recent alterations and extensions to the building. These alterations have provided an extension to the restaurant business of the pub but left the bar area materially unchanged. The tiled floor is dotted with solid chairs and tables, complemented by comfortable wall seats both in the main bar area and the tiny side room. A feature of the pub is a large fireplace, the chimneybreast of which is decorated with a number of old flintlock shotguns. Elsewhere the ubiquitous horse brasses and varieties of copper and brass ornaments are at home in the timeless atmosphere of the room. Two people tired of this atmosphere a decade ago, however; the ghost of an old lady and child appeared regularly from the 1750's until 1980 when the pub last underwent alterations — perhaps they didn't approve, although it's hard to imagine why.

Until fairly recently a free house, the Plough is now tied to Thwaites brewery; only the bitter is currently available. The pub is open from noon to 3 pm and 6.30 pm to 11 pm, bar meals are served from noon to 2.30 pm and 6.30 pm to 9.30 pm. It is possible that all day opening may be introduced on summer Saturdays in 1991.

The Walk

Walk down the right side of the pub and through to the back of the car park beyond, cross the stile here and walk along line of the fence on the right of the narrow pasture. Cross the stile about half way along this fence and turn left, crossing a further two stiles to emerge on a minor road at the top of the bungalow's garden. Cross virtually straight over and enter the field opposite through the gate to the left of the black wooden barn. Walk ahead towards the middle of the hedge across the far end of the field, cross the small, overgrown footbridge and follow the line of hedge on your right, aiming for the isolated red brick house. Cross the stile and walk up the right hand side of the house, go through the gate at the front and turn right along the drive.

Walk along this past further houses on your right, cross through the rickety gate and continue on along the green track beyond. At the end of the first field on your left is a stile, climb this and walk ahead across the field to the tow-path of the Lancaster Canal, turning right along this. The canal is your companion for the next mile or so, lined here and there with trees or tall rushbeds and heavily populated by all sorts of water birds. Even in summer this canal is fairly peaceful, largely because it is landlocked (it always has been, plans to link it to the Ribble in Preston never came to fruition). Views off to your left encompass Longridge Fell, the southern fells of The Forest of Bowland and the outlying, wooded, Beacon Fell. Remain on the tow-path until you reach the bridge next to the feed mill, climb off the tow-path here and then cross the bridge, walking along with the main road into the village of Woodplumpton.

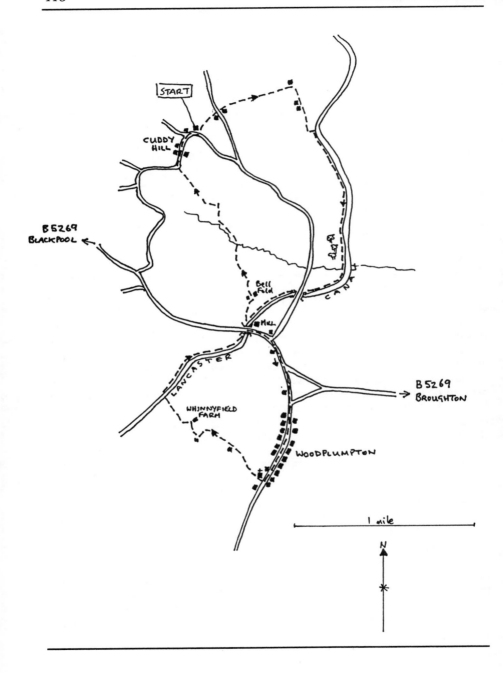

Woodplumpton

This long linear village is no more than a veneer on each side of the Preston road; it is recorded in Domesday but few of the buildings in today's village can claim a long history. An exception is St. Anne's Church, a curious mixture of trim, Georgian style architecture and much older, weather-beaten sandstone which may date back to the Thirteenth century. The village stocks remain in place just outside the lychgate, next door is a farm dated 1702 and opposite is the village pub The Wheatsheaf (Matthew Brown, bar snacks). A curious burial in the churchyard is that of Meg Shelton, the Fylde witch. She was a local villager, Margery Hilton, who had been saddled with a tarnished and unholy reputation. When she died in 1705 she was buried at the dead of night but, come the following morning, had scratched her way out of her grave. A second burial met with the same result so the third attempt included the variation of burying her face-down and capping the grave with a large boulder. This has apparently worked as the boulder remains undisturbed beside a path in the churchyard.

The walk leaves the village via the churchyard. Walk west through the churchyard, passing Megs grave on your left and turn right at the crossing of paths. Climb down through the gap in the graveyard wall at the end of this path and walk ahead and slightly left, picking up the hedge on your right. Walk along through the fields, keeping the hedge to your right. At the end of the fields go through the gate and turn left along the drive, winding round with it and passing two houses on your left to reach the farmyard at Whinnyfield Farm. Walk up the farmyard past the barn on your left and the bull pen to your right and, at the far end, turn left along the muddy track. Go through the gate, pass the barn to your left and follow the track for a few yards more, then turning right along the track across the field. At the end of this cross the canal bridge and then rejoin the tow-path, walking this time with the water on your right.

Walk alongside the canal back to the bridge beside the feed mill. Immediately before this bridge turn left, cross the stile at the end of the short track and then walk up the road to the canal bridge. Do not cross it but turn left, then left again in a matter of yards and walk along the drive to Bell Fold Farm. Walk through the unusually tidy farmyard, pass through the gate at the far end and go along the track beyond. At the end of this track go through the gate and walk across the field ahead, aiming a few yards to the right of the pylon. Cross the wide wooden bridge over the stream at the far side of this field and turn left, walking alongside New Mill Brook.

Pass by the point where some rusty pipes arch across the stream, cross into the next field and then turn right, following the hedge on your right around the edge of the field. You'll eventually reach a stile beneath an oak tree, cross this and the plank bridge beyond, then walk along the right hand edge of the field. In a short while cross a further small footbridge and then walk ahead to the end of the field just a few yards to the left of the barn and corrugated iron sheds. Climb the stile here (just behind the chevron) and turn right along the road, winding round with this back to the pub about three hundred yards away.

Lancaster Canal, Woodplumpton

16. CENTRAL LANCASHIRE: WADDINGTON

Route: Waddington – West Bradford – Ribble Way – Grindleton – Cuttock Clough

Distance: 7 Miles

Map: Sheet SD 64/74 Clitheroe and Chipping

Start: The Buck Inn, Waddington

Access: Waddington is on the B6478 road about two miles to the north of Clitheroe on the Slaidburn road. The Buck Inn is just behind St. Helens Church near the top of the village, not to be confused with the Upper Buck Inn in the tiny square at the top of the one long main street. Parking is very restricted both at the pub and in the village as a whole.

The Buck Inn (0200 28705)

The Buck contributes directly to keeping the local hospital and almshouses going. Not, as in many a local pub, via collection boxes, sponsored dwyle flonking or potty hurling contests but through the rental on the property paid by licensee Jim Brown to a trust which actually owns the pub. The trust also supports the village hospital, hence the connection. The trust was established centuries ago by the Parker family, who still live at nearby Browsholme Hall, a powerful Lancashire family who once held the title Bowbearers of the Forest of Bowland, a leading function in medieval times.

The pub is a listed building thanks largely to the simple early Victorian glasswork incorporated into the pub's solid wooden bar surround. This bar splits the pub into its two main rooms. The main, front room houses a well used piano and is warmed by a red-polished brick surround fire. The old flag flooring is now carpeted over but a solid, carved sideboard as old as the pub (1760) remains recessed into the wall. The back room is the locals tap room, like the main room simply but comfortably furnished reflecting the congenial atmosphere of this old village social centre.

The Buck Inn, Waddington

Most importantly the bar itself is furnished with four handpumps used to dispense Wards Bitter (Sheffield), Robinsons Best Bitter (Stockport), Tetleys Bitter and Tim Taylors Best Bitter(Keighley). The range may vary from time to time but, as Jim says, if it sells it will remain on.

The Buck largely retains the atmosphere and character of the small coaching inn it once was. It was built for the Parker family who have an interest to this day through the board of trustees; some of the roof beams in the front bar are said to be from Browsholme Hall. Two of the old inn bedrooms are still let out to visitors, a third is an a la carte restaurant. The original coach house survives beside the pub, retaining its original doors and massive wooden swivel hinge whilst behind the pub the stables are still standing. The old bell pull still functions in the third of the pub's public rooms; now used as a children's room; it too has a fine old fireplace and woodwork. As befits coaching inn days there are no electronic games or musical treats.

Joyce Brown is in charge of the catering, all home produced and cooked food available seven days a week and including a renowned Sunday roast. Food is available from noon to 3 pm and 7.15 pm to 10.30 pm; the pub itself is open 11 am to 3 pm and 6 am to 11 pm on Mondays to Wednesdays and all day Thursdays to Saturdays.

Waddington

The village brook tumbles down through the entire length of the village, hemming in the main street which crosses and recrosses the water as and where it can, threading its way between brookside and cottage gardens which are a riot of colour for most of the year. Venerable old cottages line either side of this surprisingly wide main thoroughfare, leading up to the tiny square at the head of the village where bull baiting was once a favourite local "sport." The medieval church of St. Helen's, largely rebuilt in late Victorian times, stands down a lane off the main street next to the old smithy, the village stocks and the pinfold, where stray cattle and pigs were once impounded. Across the stream is Waddington Old Hall, home to the family after whom the village is named. Henry 6 took refuge here following defeat at the Battle of Hexham during the Wars of the Roses. He was informed upon however, and fled only to be captured nearby a few days later and ignominiously transported to the Tower of London tied, facing backwards, to the back of a mule. The Hall can be viewed from the road but is not open to the public.

CENTRAL LANCASHIRE

The Ribble river is the heart and soul of Central Lancashire. From its source high in the Three Peaks area of North Yorkshire it sweeps in a wide swathe through the County effectively cutting it in two, separating the great northern fortress of upland Bowland from the moorland bloc of the West Pennines in the south, the northern lowlands of Amounderness from the Lancashire Plain. It is the only river to flow westwards from the Yorkshire Dales, its source little more than a stone's throw from that of that most famous of Dales rivers, the Wharfe.

Entering Lancashire with a flourish in a deep, wooded valley near Gisburn it is throughout its length overshadowed by outlying fells – Longridge, Grindleton, Pendle Hill and Mellor Moor (all of which I include in this generous definition of Central Lancashire). The steep valley sides and terraces are dappled with isolated hamlets and small villages, linked by a latticework of country lanes, tracks and greenways and virtually undisturbed by major roads. These small settlements are familiar to many – although few could name them – as they often feature in national travel and tourism guides and magazines, representative of that quintessential idyll, the English country village untouched by the passage of time.

There are only two towns of any size in the whole valley, Preston at its estuary and Clitheroe, the old Norman fortress town guarding the central Ribble Valley. These, together with Roman Ribchester and the old Abbey settlement at Sawley are the only places with any river frontage to speak of. The rest is a mixture of pastureland, country estates and woodland, crossed by an occasional road but largely disturbed only by the Ribble Way footpath which is waymarked for virtually the whole length of the river. The only blot on this otherwise idyllic landscape is the cement works near Clitheroe, an infamous landmark and the only industrial intrusion of any scale in the valley upstream of Preston. This guarantees a largely unpolluted watercourse reflected in a run of salmon and sea trout matched only by the Lune in the far north of Lancashire.

There could hardly be a greater contrast to this riverscape than that other great feature of Central Lancashire, the sharp-profiled and isolated fells typified by the windswept Longridge Fell and Pendle Hill, infamous not only for its connections with witchcraft but also for sudden squalls and heavy downpours which materialize suddenly out of the clearest of skies. These outlying knuckles of Carboniferous age sandstone and gritstone have proved more resistant to erosion than neighbouring shale deposits resulting in these local extremes of topography.

The Walk

From The Buck turn left, walk along past St. Helen's Church and down to the main street. Cross straight over both this and the stream and turn left uphill, the Sun Inn on your immediate right. At the top turn right, you'll almost immediately see the hospital and almshouses off to your left. For the next mile you must remain with this minor road – the path across the fields is blocked by new housing – to reach the village of West Bradford. The road is quiet, however, and furnishes good views to Pendle Hill, somewhat tarnished by the cement work chimneys.

Pass the Three Millstones pub and then turn right along the track which follows the stream down into the village – walk along with the stream on your left. At the end of this track/path bear left past the cottage and walk along the front of the short terrace. On gaining the village street turn right and walk downhill. The old mill, now being converted into luxury apartments, was in use until 1960, initially as a corn mill then a cotton mill. Continue down the hill out of the village, looking at the

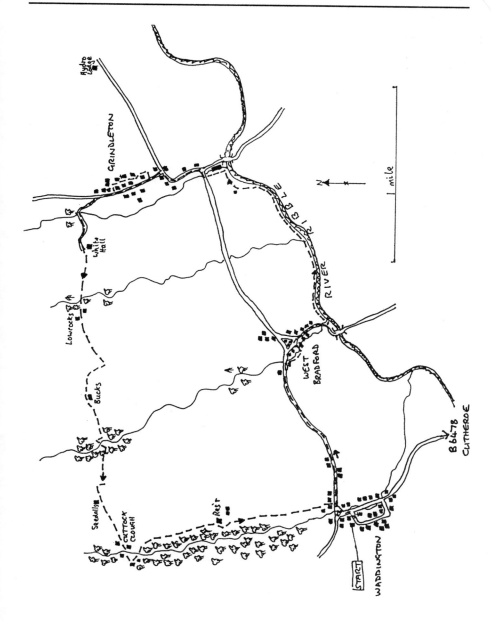

bottom for a public footpath sign on the left pointing towards Grindleton. Go over the stile here and join the riverside walk, a part of the Ribble Way. Remain with the riverbank and walk upstream, crossing stiles and footbridges as necessary. At one point the path leaves the river at a meander and cuts across the neck of land. Pass the small sewage works on your left here then cross the concrete bridge over the sidestream, rejoining the riverbank and walking towards the long, low mill ahead.

Before you reach the mill look up to your left to spot a flight of steps and a stile beneath a large beech tree. Leave the riverbank here, climb the steps and walk along the fenced path to the road at the far end of the row of cottages. Turn right and wind uphill with the road to the village of Grindleton. Turn left up the road beside the Duke of York pub, a reminder that the village was, until 1984, in Yorkshire. You're now walking up Main Street, one of two parallel village streets. The other one, Back Lane, is off to your right and is an unmade track, worth seeking out to find the large Methodist chapel half way up. Old cottages line both these roads which climb steeply up from the Ribble Valley.

Continue up Main Street, passing the bus turning area to reach the fork at the top of the village; bear left here, opposite Whinside House, and walk steeply downhill to the brook. On your right you'll pass a small calcite chute formed at the outlet of a land drain. This has been formed by the very hard water depositing some of its load of dissolved lime in solution, in just the same way as stalactites and stalagmites form in limestone caves. Grindleton was once renowned as a minor health spa, the lime and sulphur rich waters could be taken at the Hydro Hotel to the east of the village or at Wortwells Well near White Hall. To reach White Hall just remain with the road, cross Grindleton Brook and wind uphill again. Pass the Hall on your left and walk on for a further hundred yards or so. Turn right, cross the cattle grid and then bear left at a shallow angle up the field, aiming for a stile half way along the wire fence ahead of you. Cross this, and the further stile visible ahead, walking towards the distant transmitter to cross a further stile beside two thorn trees. Once across this walk to the far side of the field and turn left down the sunken track to the stream, crossing the footbridge here. Walk up the far side, favouring the left hand path and cross the field at the crest of the dingle, then pass through the gate beside the new barn.

Follow the track up past the farm on your left and walk through the farmyard, leaving at the far end over the cattle grid. Remain on the surfaced drive which contours Simpsley Hill and turn right at the junction, crossing a further two cattle grids in the process. Walk up this lane, bearing left at the top to reach the gate leading to Bucks Farm. Go through the gate into the yard. The right of way actually passes behind the house and barn to reach the gate you can see at the far end of the yard, although most people tend to walk in front of the farmhouse. Go through this gate and follow the line of fence and rough track ahead. Pass through the next gate and look ahead for the gate which will lead you down into the wooded valley of Drakehouse Wood. Go through this gate, bear right and follow the path down to the stream, crossing this via the boulders and walking ahead then steeply left out of the deep cleft. At the top look for the gate through the fence, slightly to your left. Pass through this and then bear half right to the short, isolated section of wall, beside which is a gate. Go through this and follow the fence on your left for about fifty yards to the line of an old wall which goes up the field to your right. At this point bear half right and walk diagonally across the field, heading for the white cottage in the distance.

Cross the cattle grid at the corner of the field and turn right up the lane, turning left at the top towards Seedalls Farm. At the end of the drive go through the gate at the sign "footpath only" and walk along the rutted track to Cuttock Clough Farm. Stay with the track through the farmyard, cross the stream and walk on up the road. Just before reaching the modern stone house on your left turn left and walk down the track with the cupressus hedge on your right. Pass the two permanent caravans and go over the little footbridge across the stream, from the far side of which walk up left to the edge of the woodland, then sticking with the woodland edge path and walking downstream. Skirt round to the right of the covered reservoir and cross directly over the track beyond. Don't go through the obvious gate but look to your right along the wall to find a high stone-step stile across the wall – it's marked by a blue hydrant sign. Once over this stile continue to follow the edge of the woods down along the long, narrow fields. Views ahead include Clitheroe, Whalley and the moors above Blackburn.

When you reach the gate at the edge of the field, at the far side of which you can see a stone barn, don't go through that gate but turn left and follow the line of fence and trees. Cross the stile beside the next gate and follow the line of trees down the field. On reaching the fence at the far side walk down the left hand side of it and follow the line of wall, which is the hospital boundary, on your right down to the bottom. Join the road at the bottom, turn right and walk the few yards back to the top of Waddington's main street.

17. CENTRAL LANCASHIRE: GOOSNARGH

Route: Goosnargh – Chingle – Longley Lane – Brook Bridge

Distance: 5.5 Miles

Map: Sheet SD 43/53 Preston (North) and Kirkham (Lancs)

Start: The Grapes Inn, Goosnargh

Access: From Preston take the A6 north for about three miles to Broughton village crossroads (or from Junction 32 on the M6 follow the Garstang signs via Junction 1 on the M55). At the traffic lights here turn right along the B5269 towards Longridge; Goosnargh is about two miles along this road. Look for the sign on the right (just before the Stags Head) directing you left into Goosnargh village and take this, Church Lane, winding through the houses to the pub which adjoins the churchyard at the far end of the village.

The Grapes Inn (0772 865234)

The pub next to the church claims a lineage going back at least to the times of The Crusades when, for obvious reasons, it was called The Saracens Head. Landlord Hugh Gregory is confident that there was an alehouse on the site at the time of Domesday in 1086. Local legend has it that during the Fifteenth Century the incumbent parish priest at the church was also the licensee of the Saracens Head; at this time an as-yet undiscovered tunnel linking the two buildings was supposedly built. It is possible that the church silverware which disappeared after the Civil War is hidden in such a tunnel; certainly Cromwell, who used the pub as a base whilst "alterations" to the church were made, came away empty-handed. Well, almost. He had the satisfaction of renaming the pub the General Elliot after one of his army commanders.

Much modernised and now called The Grapes the low beamed, multi roomed Tetleys pub offers the rambler a choice of handpumped Jennings Bitter or Boddingtons Bitter; the former is a long standing regular, the latter a guest beer recently introduced and selling well. The substantial bar is heavily laden with Toby Jugs, miner's lamps and copper oddments and serves a large, plush lounge area which also hosts a separate food counter, home cooked meals being available daily except Sundays from noon to 2 pm and 7 pm to 9.30 pm. There's a separate games room and even a tiny, hidden snug accessible only through the bar and used, it is said, by the parish priest in centuries past to enjoy a tipple out of the gaze of any parishioners who may have been on a similar mission. The pub boasts a Crown Green bowling green, one of a large number in the area, and is renowned during the summer months for its plethora of colourful, even gaudy, hanging baskets. Landlord Hugh Gregory is a mine of information about local history and the local area; try and pin him down between noon to 3 pm or 6 pm to 11 pm.

The Grapes Inn, Goosnargh

Goosnargh

The name evidences the Scandinavian origins of the village; *nargh* can mean field or clearing in a wood, obviously one where geese were once penned. The history of the whole area reeks of past invaders. The land from the hills east of the village to the coast at what is now Blackpool was once known as Amounderness. Amound was King of the Vikings and the shape of the coastline in those early days was likened to that of the King's nose – Amounderness, Amound's nose. Viking ships are known to have been wrecked off the coast and analysis of old timbers in the ancient village church of St. Mary the Virgin reveal that they are impregnated with sea salt and date from the tenth century, possibly timbers from wrecks on the shifting coastline just a few miles from the village.

That old triumvirate of village church, manor and pub close together is alive and well in Goosnargh. In fact there are two pubs, The Grapes and The Bushells Arms opposite, named after the Bushell family, squires of the manor, who lived in the imposing early Georgian mansion, dated 1722, which adjoins the churchyard. The last squire was Dr. William Bushell. He outlived both his wife and daughter and, ahead of his time, established his mansion as a hospital for the use of "decayed gentlefolk" resident within a six mile radius of Preston. A trust set up on his death in 1735 ensures that this stipulation remains to this day; another stipulation is that residents have four meals a day with beer at one meal and ale at another.

The village has another hospital at Whittingham Hall. This psychiatric hospital was once the second largest of its kind in Europe and totally self sufficient with seven estate farms supplying food and materials for building and clothing; it even had its own railway line and station on a spur off the now closed Preston to Longridge line. Now being rapidly run down its future lies as an upmarket country club and exclusive housing development after final closure in 1994.

Much of Goosnargh today is modern housing to the west of the old village core, largely now a dormitory town for Preston. One building, however, predates all but the church. Chingle Hall, a small, white-washed brick building with the remains of a moat about a mile to the south of the village, was built in 1260. It now holds claim to be the most haunted house in Britain, spectres include St. John Wall, a headless martyr. There are no less than four priest holes in this, the oldest brick built domestic building still standing in Britain. The Hall is open to the public daily between 10 am and 5 pm.

The Walk

Leaving The Grapes walk straight ahead, The Bushells Arms on your right, the mansion to the left. Where the road bends sharply left at the far end of the mansion's garden carry straight ahead along the rough track for a few yards and then turn right along the driveway leading to Bushells Cottage. Skirt the lawn on your right, the cottage to your left and walk beneath the oak tree in the rough garden beyond. Look for the stile on the right, cross this and turn left to follow the line of hedge. Carry straight on across the field where this hedge bends left, aiming for the modern house to the left of a clump of trees at the far side of the field. These trees surround a pond; walk round the left side of this pond, cross the stile and walk up along the narrow, overgrown path up to the main road, turning right along this.

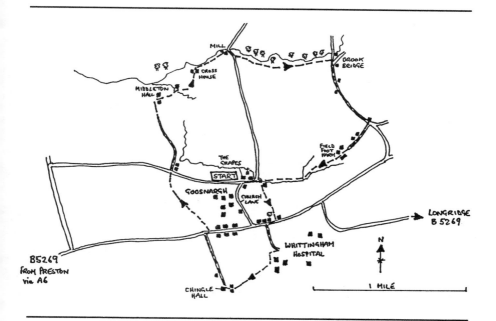

Within about a hundred yards take the road on the left into the grounds of Whittingham Hospital and bear left with it, looking on your right for a stile beside the white painted gate. Cross this stile and walk to the copse of trees ahead, skirting the right edge of these (whilst remaining on the copse side of the fence) until you reach a concrete stile. Climb this and turn left, walking along to the far end of the long, low red brick barn. Remain on your side of the fence at the end and turn right following the fence, then a hedge, along two fields, crossing stiles as appropriate. A further stile takes you across a wire fence, from here head half right to pass between the two barns (one brick, one sandstone) and turn right along the farm drive. The white building on your left here is Chingle Hall, the remains of a moat visible beside and behind the building; a short bridged causeway leads to the front entrance. Remain with the farm drive and walk to the main road at its end.

Turn right along the road and then, in less than fifty yards, take the signposted footpath off to the left, opposite a bus stop sign. Cross the stile and walk along the left edge of the field, entering the succeeding field via a stone slab stile and following the line of hedge on your right. Pass the old brick building to your left and walk along the muddy farm track to the minor road at the end. Cross directly over this and walk down the lane opposite, a directional bridleway sign indicating Longley Lane. Remain with this for about a mile. The ridge dominating the horizon ahead is the line of Bleasdale Moors, the highest point is Fair Snape Fell, at over 1600 feet one of the highest points in Lancashire; nearer to hand is the wooded knoll of Beacon Fell.

On reaching the complex of buildings that is Middleton Hall Farm turn right to walk between a brick pillared barn on the left and some silo's on your right. The path then passes the foot of the lawn leading up to the farmhouse to reach a stile. Climb this and remain with the hedge and deep ditch to your left; where the hedge bends sharp left you should head half left to cross a stream beneath an Elm tree. Walk up the bank opposite, keeping the sparse hedge to your left, winding round at the top and following the wire fence to emerge on a farm drive beside a big new barn. Walk along the drive keeping the barn on your left then bear right into the farmyard of Cross House Farm. After only a few yards turn left and walk along with a wooden rail fence on your left and the high concrete wall surrounding the farmhouse on your right. Walk down the hill to the stream and take the stile on the right just before reaching the footbridge, skirting the bottom of the farm's garden. Cross a further stile and then follow the water for several hundred yards.

On the opposite bank major engineering work has been undertaken to prevent bank collapse. Soon after this, on your bank, look for a stile hidden behind a large fallen tree, virtually next to the water. Climb this, follow the water for a short distance then bear right with the path into a cultivated garden passing a greenhouse to your left, sheds to your right. Ahead is the redeveloped Goosnargh Mill, on the left the mill house itself. Walk through the yard between these two buildings and along the drive to the road, turning right here to walk a short distance uphill. Where the road bends right take the stile on the left into the field and walk ahead along the river terrace, a rough hedge to your left beyond which is the old mill leat and beyond this the stream. Cross the next stile between two thorn bushes and remain parallel to the river. The site of the old weir supplying the leat is vaguely discernible down to your left, at which point the stream arcs away left; you should remain on a straight heading and walk to the tall oak tree at the far left corner of the field.

Walk to the left of this tree, keep the hedge to your right and then leave the field via the stile at the far end. Cross the track and climb the substantial wooden stile opposite, a few yards further on the stream reappears on your left. Pass beneath the line of pylons and walk along the edge of the field towards the stone house in the distance at Brook Bridge. Climb down to the minor road and turn right along it, bearing right again at the junction to walk along Eaves Green Lane. Stay with this for the next half mile or so, passing several houses en route including the fine Brook Cottage on your left. Opposite an ivy clad cottage, and before the road bends sharply right, turn right along the drive towards Field Foot Farm – you can't miss it as there's a large fawn coloured sign-board.

Walk along to the farm, passing two bungalows on your right. On reaching the complex of farm buildings walk straight ahead, battery houses to both sides, silos to your left, then to your right. Enter the field at the far end and bear right, crossing through a further field gate and then turn left. Walk along the line of the hedge to your left, cross a stile and then follow the stream to a footbridge. Cross this, turn right and look for a further footbridge (simply a stone slab) about a hundred yards along. Recross the stream here and turn left, following the course of the stream. At the end of the field cross the stile (about twenty yards upfield from the stream) and walk across the meadow to a further stile by a gate. Climb this, turn left and follow the driveway around to the road, from which point The Grapes is visible in the distance.

18. CENTRAL LANCASHIRE: HOLDEN

Route: Holden – Bolton-by-Bowland – Bolton Park – Sawley – Till House

Distance: 6 Miles

Map: Sheet SD 64/74 Clitheroe and Chipping

Start: The Copy Nook Hotel, Holden, Bolton-by-Bowland

Access: Holden is a hamlet immediately west of Bolton-by-Bowland, about six miles north-east of Clitheroe. Join the A59 and drive towards Skipton. About three miles beyond Clitheroe (which the A59 bypasses to the south) turn left at the sign to Sawley and Bolton-by-Bowland; look for the brown road sign for Sawley Abbey. Wind through Sawley, cross the river bridge and bear right towards Bolton. The Copy Nook is a further two miles along this road, on the left at a sharp bend and junction.

The Copy Nook Hotel (02007 205)

Keep your wits about you if you're at the Copy Nook on New Year's Day as there's an odd – some may say sadistic – custom enacted nearby. Tradition has it that battle be entered against locals from the Coach and Horses in nearby Bolton-by-Bowland; the fight is to the bitter end, bitter being the operative word as the battle is a tug of war held across the Beck in Bolton; the losers end up bitter(ly) cold and wet. This long standing tradition is taken seriously; there's a picture of the victorious Copy Nook team of 1918 – 20 in the bar, who knows how many unsuspecting ramblers have been roped into taking part in the past.

Such "bitter" drinkers then return to the bar to tussle with their next challenge, which of the nest of handpumps to choose first. There's usually a choice of Theakstons Best Bitter, Websters Yorkshire Bitter, Ruddles County and Timothy Taylors Landlord. An occasional guest beer may displace one of these regulars, particularly during the winter when an old ale may be available; a recent favourite was the quaintly named "Old Fart" from the Robinwood Brewery in Todmorden (maybe a tactical ploy by Landlord Roger Jowett to put the wind up the opposition's tug of war team....).

The history of the pub has been lost in the mists of time, as has the origin of its name. Until late last century it was, like many in the area, a working farm-cum-pub. It's now a small country house hotel and Free House with a growing reputation for the quality of its food as well as its selection of beers. There's a cosy atmosphere in the open plan bar area; in their two years there Roger and Pru Jowett have built a strong local following, recently enhanced (if that's the right word) by the "adoption" of the Clitheroe Morris Men who practice their mysterious rites and rituals at the Copy Nook most Sundays; full dress rehearsals and performances are promised for the summer.

You'll find the Copy Nook open from 11 am to 3 pm and 6 pm to 11 pm, food (all home prepared using local produce and stock) is served each lunchtime (noon to 2 pm) and evening (7 pm to 9.30 pm except Mondays).

The Walk

The route of this walk near Till House Farm is very ambiguous, the route recommended here is based on the evidence of home-made waymarking and of previous walkers.

The walk also involves fording the river near Bolton-by-Bowland. When you enter the village note the condition of the water. If it is clear and/or low then you'll have no problem with the fording. If, however, the river is dirty and high then the ford will be impassable and you should take the alternative route outlined.

Turn left out of the pub and left again to walk up the narrow road beside the pub towards Slaidburn. In a few hundred yards you'll reach Holden itself, a huddle of cottages on the banks of the deeply incised Holden Beck. Bear left at the junction and cross the bridge over the Beck, then turn immediately left along the track and pass by the end of the old pack horse bridge. Go through the left hand gate and walk along the pastureside above the river; down to your left is a spectacular waterfall whilst slightly upstream the water tumbles over a series of natural stone steps.

Follow Holden Beck downstream, cross the stile and remain with the river for a further fifty yards or so, then bear right and walk over to the far right hand corner of the field, in line with the road you can see climbing a short bank. At the corner cross the stile and descend the steep steps, then follow the road right and up the hill to reach Bolton Peel

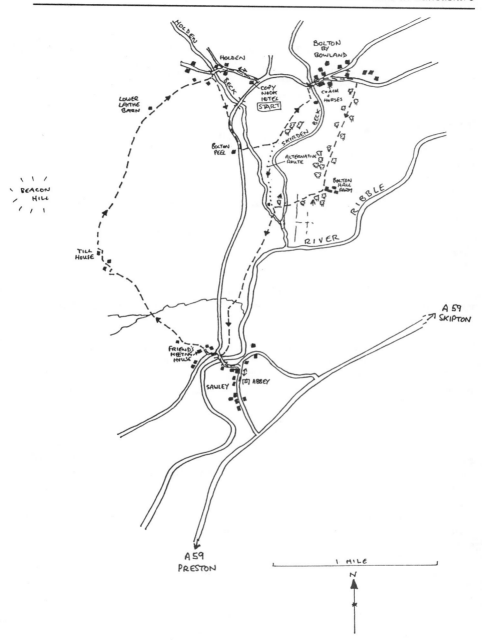

Farm on your right, a fine solid old farmhouse with an old cross in front of it beside the road. Opposite the entrance to the farmyard and on your left a stone step stile takes you over the wall, thence scramble down the steep slope and walk to the footbridge over the Beck. Cross this and head slightly right across the field, passing about ten yards to the right of the telegraph pole and climbing the river terrace to the stile over the wire fence – it takes a little finding, so persevere.

Once across this walk in line of sight towards the white house on the distant hillside. Cross the next stile and then walk along the line of fence off to your left, beyond which is a pond. Beside the isolated oak tree on the ridge top is the base of an old cross, from here walk down to the corner of the field with the sheep pens and dip. Cross the stile here then walk virtually straight ahead up the long farm drive to its end, turn right and cross the bridge to walk into Bolton-by-Bowland.

Bolton-by-Bowland

Yorkshire, of which the village was a part until 1974, is famous for its village greens; Bolton-by-Bowland has two of them. The lower, smaller one retains a thirteenth century market cross and the village stocks and is bordered by Kirk Beck, a smattering of cottages and the village inn, The Coach and Horses. I'd like to report on this but have yet to find it open on a weekday lunchtime; it advertises cask ale – Castle Eden, I believe – and has a good reputation for food so I hope your luck is better than mine. The village's one main street, lined at its western end with terraces of tiny cottages which retain mounting blocks and a solid external staircase, winds between the two greens past one of the village centre farms which remain the heart of the community.

The village church of St Peter and St Paul stands on the hillside between the two greens. It, too, dates back to the thirteenth century and its features include a hagioscope, or leper's squint, through which such unfortunates could watch a service, and a massive studded oak door complete with well worn wooden sanctuary bar, used to block the door from within by those seeking sanctuary in the church. There is also a list of Rectors going back to 1304; two of them gave exceptional service, William Pudsay from 1448 to 1507 and Richard Dawson from 1773 to 1826. The most impressive feature, however, is the tomb of Sir Ralph Pudsay in the Chantry Chapel. He had three wives and twenty five children; the relief-tomb depicts all these with the number of children each wife gave him carved in roman numerals at the feet of the appropriate wife.

Sir Ralph lived at the now-demolished Bolton Hall (it burned down earlier this century) and offered sanctuary there to Henry 6 after the Battle of Hexham in 1464. It is said that the King whiled away some of his short time there in redesigning the tower of the church, the results of which may be seen today. The village's other, larger green lies to the east of the church, a massive open area bounded by buildings which include the old courthouse where guardians of the ancient Forest Laws used to decide on rights of residence in the Forest of Bowland.

If the water in the river is clear and low then leave the village along the long, tree lined drive, opposite the church, that once led to Bolton Hall. Cross over the ridge and walk down to the white gate at the edge of the woodland, marked by a notice "Private BHE". This is the public footpath so go through the gate and wind along through the plantation to emerge in a large grass covered yard at the far end of which is a white cottage at the end of a line of barns. Turn right down the track at your side of this grassed area and pass through the gate at the bottom. From here turn right, pass to the right of the stand of trees in the field and walk ahead to the river, aiming in line of sight for the left hand end of the line of oak and scots pine woodland on the terrace ahead, crossing an awkward and wide drainage ditch en route. Fording the river is easy at this point, just use the lines and humps of stones and pebbles and wade through water only two or three inches deep. Once on the far bank pass to the left of the line of trees and walk left along the terrace to the footbridge.

Alternative route

If the water is dirty or higher than normal then retrace your steps from Bolton-by-Bowland, recross the river bridge and turn left down the farm drive, enter the field by the sheep pens and walk up to the base of the old cross by the oak tree. Cross the stile in the fence beyond this and then join the woodland edge on the left. Bend gradually round left with this and then walk straight across the fields ahead, crossing stiles as necessary and join the stream on your right. Pass the line of oak and pine on your left, climb the stile out of the field just beyond these trees and walk ahead along the terrace to the footbridge mentioned above.

Cross the footbridge and bear half left to cross the stile between the two gnarled old oak trees. Walk to the far right hand corner of the field you are now in, heading essentially for the low hilltop in the valley ahead. Cross the stile at this corner and then follow the riverbank along to the next stile. Climb this and then follow the line of white stones across the field – the path doesn't follow the riverbank. If it is frosty or snowing then the stones won't be obvious; your line of travel is at a shallow tangent to the right away from the riverbank which will bring you to a sleeper bridge across a stream about half way down the right hand edge of the field. Cross this and turn left, remaining with the line of hedge on your right until you reach the bridge at Sawley. It's worthwhile making a short detour here to visit Sawley, so cross the bridge and walk along to the village, bearing sharp right at the Spread Eagle Hotel.

Sawley

A compact little village huddled beneath the steep slopes of Noddle Hill, Sawley owes its existence to William de Percy who, in 1148, endowed a Cistercian Abbey on the narrow floodplain of the Ribble here at Salley, translated as "Land of the Willows." The founding monks came from the massive Fountains Abbey. It was an ideal spot for a Cistercian community, the White Monks were renowned for their agricultural and fish farming skills and a small but thriving community survived until the Dissolution in 1536 when it was recorded as being the poorest religious House in Yorkshire (in which County it was until 1974), largely due to its proximity to the larger Whalley Abbey just a few miles away. In the following centuries the Abbey buildings were severely vandalised to provide building stone for local projects – the barn by the river bridge, for example, has obviously relied on such stone – resulting in the scant remains which line the side of the village road today. The few surviving walls and arches are a shadow of its former glories, surrounding field marks and crop marks give a far better impression of the complete settlement. The Abbey, to which admission is free, is closed on Mondays.

Surprisingly the village no longer has a church or chapel, although there is a Quaker Meeting Room across the river. There was once a calico printworks in the village but this was closed just after the Napoleonic Wars; the building then saw use as a Methodist chapel before being converted into three-storey cottages. By-passed by the busy A59, Sawley is now a tranquil backwater and a favourite stop for walkers on the Ribble Way which passes through the village.

Return to and re-cross the river bridge and go left at the junction a few yards further on. In a short while turn right up the narrow road leading up to the Friends (Quakers) Meeting House. At the end go into the driveway of Green End Cottage and walk round to the left of the garage to reach the field gate at the top of the garden, cross through this and then, as the notice suggests, follow the white markers across the fields for the next half mile or so. Some are more obvious than others and may be painted on trees or fenceposts, be white plastic container bottoms tied to bushes or bits of old white porcelain sinks.

After about half a mile these markers seem to disappear. The last one you'll come to is in the top right hand corner of the field after you cross a footbridge over the Sliping Brook. Once over the stile marked by this last white board stick to the left of the field and walk uphill, crossing the stile in the top left hand corner of this field and the subsequent one a few yards further on. From here the way is not at all obvious, I've followed the tracks left by previous walkers as a guide.

Once over the last stile bear three-quarters right to the gap in the wall and join the rough track at the corner here below the barn and farmhouse. Walk down the track for a few yards, climb the rail fence across it and then climb the bank on the left to the metal gate. Pass through this and walk across the pasture to the small barn, passing to the left of this to reach a farm driveway, then turning right up this. The right of way here passes behind the farmhouse but when I last did the walk chalked arrows and white markers led up through the farmyard so this is the route I followed. Wind through the yard and up the drive beyond for a few yards to the point where it bends to the left. Here, straight ahead of you, rough stone steps climb the wall to a stile. Cross this stile and follow the field boundary straight ahead. At the end of this field cross the stile and walk slightly right across the shallow valley and rough pasture ahead to the further stile which is at the corner of the wire fence on the banktop ahead. Just before you reach this you cross one of the old greenways that crisscross this area, Rodhill Lane.

Views from this point stretch across Ribblesdale to the distinctive shape of Pendle Hill and well up the meandering, wooded valley of the Ribble; to your left the start of the higher fells above Grindleton. Once over the stile walk roughly in line with the fence on your left, falling away very gently downhill to cross another stile barely fifteen yards downslope from the top fence. Continue to work gently down to the break of slope and then remain at this level along the hillside. Pass above a spring marked by a holly tree and then cross through a field gate some distance ahead. At the far side of this next field go through the gate marked by an old sink and then head for the isolated barn at Lower Laithe.

Cross the stile to the right of the barn-yard and walk on to the field gate at the far side, go through this then follow the sunken track/stream down to the stile and gate. Beyond the gate walk straight ahead towards the hamlet of Holden; keep to the right of the hedge and, once past the end of this, aim to walk past the lone oak tree then down to the bottom right corner where the farm track curves away out of the field. About fifteen yards to the right of the gate and cattle grid at this corner is a small stone stile at a gap in the line of holly bushes. Climb over this and walk a couple of paces to your right up the lane to the bend. Here go through the field gate on your left and walk down the field to the barn. Cross the stile in the left hand corner and walk down the track away from the barn, currently up for sale and conversion. Go through the gate at the end and along to the road, turn right, cross the bridge and bear right at the junction to return to the Copy Nook.

Sawley Abbey

19. CENTRAL LANCASHIRE: RIBCHESTER

Route: Ribchester – Stydd – Duddel Brook – Knowle Green – Buckley Gate

Distance: 8 Miles

Map: Sheet 680 Longridge and Great Harwood

Start: The White Bull, Ribchester.

Access: Ribchester is on the banks of the Ribble about nine miles east of Preston and four miles north of Blackburn. From Preston take the A59 towards Clitheroe and Skipton. At the traffic lights in Clayton-le-Dale (about three miles past Samlesbury aerodrome) turn left along the B6245 signposted to Ribchester. From Blackburn take the A666 towards Whalley and Clitheroe, turning onto the B6245 (signposted to Ribchester) in Wilpshire. Park in the large free car park in Ribchester, walk back to the entrance to the car park road and turn right along Church Street. The White Bull is about thirty yards along on your left.

The White Bull (0254 878303)

A pub since 1707, the building was previously Ribchester's Courthouse; when the justice donned the black cap the executions were carried out in Gallows Lane, just round the corner. The grand facade is greatly enhanced by the massive porch which is supported on four stone pillars. These pillars are said to be from the Roman Temple to Minerva which once stood some distance away; they were found in the river and recycled by the enterprising courthouse builders. Above this porch the imposing pub sign looms large, a carved wooden white bull hanging proud above the street. The pub fronts one side of the village's tiny square, other sides are hemmed in by old terraces and cottages, most of which have Roman stonemason's work incorporated into their fabric.

Inside, the pub is furnished rather like a country house hotel, comfortable seating and reserved wall decorations, largely old prints, dot the main bar area. There's a small, separate games room and a large dining area – licensee David Maginn has forged an excellent reputation for the quality and range of food available, catering for both carnivores and vegetarians alike. One carnivore that won't be eating at the pub, however, is a fox; look ahead up the stairs as you enter the pub to catch my drift. Food is available each lunchtime and on all but Monday evenings. There's a beer garden at the back which gives extensive views up the Ribble, over to Pendle Hill and across the site of the old Roman Bath House, immediately behind the pub, an excellent location in which to enjoy the Boddingtons or Chesters Bitters on offer, an occasional guest beer adds to this choice. The White Bull is open from 11.30 am to 3 pm and 6.30 pm to 11 pm.

Ribchester

Asterix, or at least his British counterparts, would have felt at home here on the Celtic fringe of the Roman Empire. The Romans took over the site of a bronze-age settlement and, in about A.D.70, established a major fort and outpost which they named Bremetennacum Veteranorum on the road from (present day) Manchester to Lancaster. Largely garrisoned first by Spanish and then Hungarian cavalry troops – subjects of the Empire rather than Romans *per se* – the fort survived until the Romans withdrew from the north in the fourth century. Patterns of trade developed and the invaders intermingled with the local Brigantes tribe, remaining in the area after the collapse of the Roman Empire.

Much of the fort has either been washed away by the changing course of the Ribble or is buried beneath the thirteenth century St. Wilfred's church and churchyard, but you can visit the old granaries and the bath-house. The Temple to Minerva, source of the White Bull's columns, is thought to have been at or near the site of the present church; the columns were recovered from the Ribble at this point. An excellent museum near the church details the Roman history of the town; exhibits include a copy of the best preserved ceremonial helmet ever found in Britain, inevitably the original is in London's British Museum. The Museum in Ribchester is open daily between March and October and on Sunday afternoons only during the winter.

Town is perhaps too grand a word to apply to the pleasant large village which exists today. A few streets of long, low, gritstone and sandstone cottages cluster round Church Street and Water Street, meeting at the tiny square outside the White Bull and interlinked by winding ginnels. More modern development lingers on the fringes beyond the Blackburn road and the villages other Bull pub, the Black Bull (Thwaites Beers, bar meals, variable lunchtime opening hours). Along Church Street and between the two Bulls is the Museum of Childhood. Based on a lifetime's collecting by the proprietors, the attractions include a flea circus, working model fairground and over 200 Teddy Bears (open daily except Mondays, 10.30 am to 5 pm).

Most of the industry – largely weaving – has long since died out to leave the village as a peaceful backwater. The Roman ford (or bridge if there ever was one) has long gone and the main road now skirts the village to a "new" bridging point a mile or so upstream. Just off this road the tiny hamlet of Stydd has a remarkable old chapel dating back to the 1100's which once belonged to the Order of the Knight's Hospitallers of St. John, one of only a handful of chapels dedicated to this Order (based in Malta) in Britain. It is kept locked and is rarely used but the low leaded windows allow a view of the austere stone-flagged, whitewashed, stone and wooden interior.

Stydd Chapel

The Walk

Turn right from the White Bull and walk along Water Street for about fifty yards, then turn right again along Greenside, winding with this to its end and passing the route to the Bath House on the way. At the end turn right along the main Blackburn Road. Pass the Ribchester Arms (Whitbread based beers, bar meals) on your left and walk along to reach Stydd Lane on the left, immediately before the bridge over the stream. Turn up this lane and follow it to its end. You pass the small church of St. Peter and St. Paul off to your left and, nearer to hand, the small but grandiose almshouses dating from 1726. Go through the farm gate at the end and walk up the drive beyond to Stydd Chapel, set in its own pastureland to your right. Remain with the track and walk up through the farmyard of Stydd Manor. At the far end leave the yard by the stile to the right of the farm gate and simply follow the rough field track up the long field beyond.

At the top right hand corner of this field are two gates. Cross the stile to the far right and bear right, passing around the top of a rough hollow and walk towards the woodland ahead, aiming for the tallest trees. Join a hedge on your right and follow this to a small enclosure of trees, immediately to the left of which are two stiles close together; cross these and continue towards the woods. Access into these woods is gained by the stile about seventy yards up from the corner; once in the woods walk down the path beyond to the stream, Duddel Brook. Cross the footbridge here, walk ahead for a few yards and then turn left along the path which parallels the stream down to your left in its deep, almost gorge like valley. In a short while you'll reach the tumbled remains of Duddel Brook (or Dutton) Mill, an old comb mill (combs for use in the woollen industry, not hair care). It's worth spending a little time exploring these remains in this spectacular setting – including the mill leat and weir upstream – before descending to the footbridges, both of which you now cross.

From the end of the second bridge follow the path gradually up the valley side to its crest. Here is a stile on your left behind an oak tree. Ignore this, and the path ahead, instead favouring the narrow path which goes steeply downhill to reach the stream; in places you'll have to scramble down rock outcrops and over fallen rocks and tree roots. You reach the stream at a very picturesque spot; to your left Duddel Brook tumbles over a waterfall into an amphitheatre-like glade whilst ahead a small brook torrents down to the main stream. Here you should ford

Duddel Brook – there are plenty of stepping stones – and climb up the valleyside opposite, bisecting the angle between the main stream and the brook. On reaching the wire fence at the top walk left to reach a stile beneath the second oak tree and cross into the field. Turn left and follow the woodland edge along to a further stile. Cross this and head half right across the field, heading for the field gate at the middle of the long hedge you are walking towards. The stile out of the field is to the right of this gate, cross it and turn left along the road.

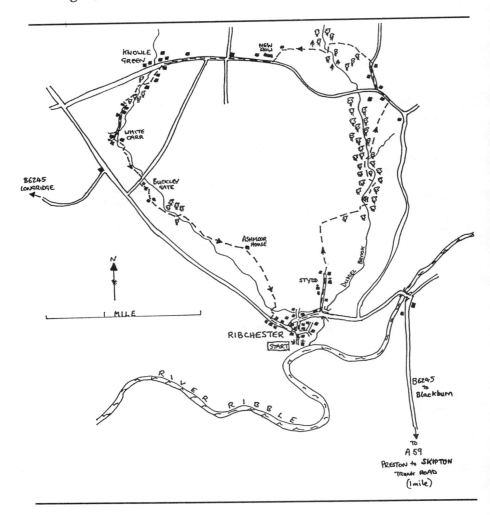

At the junction turn right up Huntington Hall Lane and follow this for about four hundred yards, passing the white cottage on your right. At the sharp bend beyond this go through the kissing gate and then head for the caravan you'll see a few hundred yards ahead. Go through the gate here, pass to the right of the caravan – Dingle Dell – and walk to the end of the paddock, just past the ruined wire enclosure. Climb the stile here and turn half left, walking now to the line of the woods at the far side of the field. Head for the tallest tree you can see, the stile into the woods is below this and leads to a path beneath a bower of rhododendron bushes. Follow this path to the driveway and turn left; cross the bridge and then take the path immediately to the right up to the kissing gate. Pass through this and then follow the woodland edge, part of the large Estate of Dutton Manor, on your right.

Where the woods end continue along the fence to the corner, cross the stile and walk to the barn about two hundred yards away. Go over the stile into the yard and then down the muddy track beyond, following this to its end just past the row of cottages, New Row. Turn right along the main road here and remain with it for nearly a mile, passing en route The Halls Arms (Whitbread) at a crossroads marking the route of the old Roman road from Ribchester to Lancaster.

On reaching the hamlet of Knowle Green look on your left for the tiny Congregational Church and adjoining Manse. A few yards downhill a driveway leads off to the left, walk along to the end of this, bearing right as necessary, to reach Clay Cottage. The drive passes to the right of the cottage and garden to end suddenly. To the right at this point descend the steep, railed steps which pass by an ivy covered ruined mill to the footbridge. Cross this bridge and bear left with the path, following it along the woodland edge. On reaching the tall stile look down to the left and climb down the slippery steps to the old barn, continuing beyond this to join the narrow road, then following this along with the stream down to your left.

On reaching the ford take the path off to the right, cross the footbridge and walk along to another ford on your left. Ahead is a footbridge, cross this and walk straight ahead passing between the rebuilt hall on your right and the renovated cottage to your left, White Carr. Enter the field ahead and walk down to the footbridge about fifty yards away. Cross this, turn left and follow the brook downstream to emerge on a narrow road about a quarter of a mile on. Turn right here then left down the drive within fifty yards to pass in front of a cottage and adjoining chicken sheds. Walk to the end of the drive and pass to the left of the house, the former Buckley Mill. At the corner here below the chimney a footbridge comes in from the left. Don't cross this but turn right, pass through the mill yard and walk across the lawn to the stile over the fence. Climb this and walk diagonally up the field beyond, climbing a further stile and then aiming for the small black cattle shed you can now see. Cross the stile to the right of this and turn left along the drive into the farmyard of Buckley Hall.

Pass straight through the farmyard, leaving by the gate beside the small barn and then walk half-left across and down the pasture, aiming for the far left hand corner marked by the gaunt skeleton of a large dead tree. Cross the stile on the left near this tree and walk down the steep slope to the footbridge. On your left the fenced off area marks the top of an old, capped, mineshaft; inspection of the riverbank below reveals evidence of shaley coal deposits. Cross the footbridge and walk ahead alongside the river. At the end of the field cross the footbridge over the sidestream, about twenty yards off the main river. Once across walk half left up the slope, passing through the obvious gaps in two old hedges. At the top bear right and walk to the isolated Ashmoor House. The path passes in front of the house, so enter the garden via the wooden fence next to the gate at the side of the house and walk along in front of the house to the drive. Remain with this, crossing two cattle grids. Some twenty yards before the next cattle grid, bounded by two stone gateposts, turn to the right. A line of stiles aligned with the chimney in Ribchester will bring you to a funnel-ended field. Here, cross the wide concrete bridge, bear half left to a stile, cross this and turn right along the track which runs beside the site of an engineering works. At the end turn left along the road and walk back into the village centre.

20. ROSSENDALE: COWPE

Route: Cowpe – Cowpe Lowe – Dearden Clough – Scout Moor – Rossendale Way – Boarsgreave

Distance: 8.5 Miles

Maps: Sheet 690 Rawtenstall and Hebden Bridge, and Sheet SD 81/91 Bury, Rochdale and Littleborough.

Start: The Buck Inn, Cowpe

Access: From Rawtenstall take the A681 road eastwards towards Bacup. In Waterfoot bear right at the traffic lights by The Railway pub and continue along Bacup Road for about a hundred yards. On the right, immediately past Barclays Bank, is the narrow Cowpe Lane – there's a picnic site signpost pointing up the road. Go up Cowpe Lane and wind around with it, pass the picnic site entrance on your right and then look for the Buck's car park on the left. The pub itself is a few yards further up the road.

The Buck Inn (0706 213612)

Cowpe Brook has cut a deep, sinuous clough into the high gritstone moors immediately south of the great trough cut by the Irwell, of which the Cowpe is a tributary. The one narrow road winds up the valley to the surviving mill at the end, lined by dark gritstone terraces, the tumbled remains of long gone mills and old lodges, hemmed in all round by the sombre moorland tops. Hardly the sort of place you'd expect to find a convivial local such as The Buck. Yet the pub survives – just – as very much of a "local's local" as the saying goes, at the same time offering a haven and a welcome for the increasing number of ramblers who are discovering this area.

I say "just" surviving as the pub isn't open on Monday to Thursday lunchtimes; landlord Peter Whittaker found it totally uneconomical so-to-do. However, Friday to Sunday lunchtimes (12 to 3) and each evening (7 to 11) finds the stack of handpumps on the bar busy dispensing Thwaites Mild and Bitter, Boddingtons Bitter and John Smiths Magnet Bitter. The pub is, essentially, two houses at the end of one of the terraces about half way up the valley. There's one large main room with an area set aside for pool and other pub games. The rest of the room is crowded with tables, stools and wall seats, warmed in the winter by a good fire in the solid, gritstone fireplace. A stag's (buck's) head stares sightlessly from his spot above this fireplace, sharing the walls with a great variety of brasses, prints, keys, spoons, lamps and similar artefacts; brass/copper kettles and scuttles adorn the fireplace. You'll find that the Buck is a great place to unwind after a long circuit of the moors; bar meals are available at weekends and children are made welcome.

ROSSENDALE

Rossendale derives its name from the old Forest of Rossendale, a royal hunting demense established for the pleasure of the Norman and Plantagenet monarchs of centuries ago. There can have been few trees even then, the acid soils and steep cloughs conspiring to ensure that the moorland heights remained the preserve of red deer and wolves, both long since gone, together with hares and rabbits to entertain the royal whim for falconry.

Present day Rossendale incorporates the Forest of Rossendale to the north of, and a swathe of high moorlands to the south of, the river Irwell which rises in the Forest, flows via Rawtenstall, Bury and the outskirts of Bolton to Salford, from where it is canalized as the Manchester Ship Canal. The Irwell's narrow valley floor is virtually infilled by high concentrations of terraced houses, mills and related industries, interspersed by areas of woodland and open spaces reclaimed from derelict mill sites. The local Groundwork Trust, one of the first to be established, has made great strides in this direction and the local authorities are doing their bit by way of establishing a regional footpath, The Irwell Valley Way. This complements the well established Rossendale Way which offers a high level circuit of the Borough of Rossendale; The Irwell Valley Way runs from the river's source above Bacup to Salford.

In centuries past this high moorland provided rich pickings for quarrymen and the area is littered with workings large and small, almost all long abandoned to nature. Old pack horse and coach routes criss-cross the tops, sunken tracks and footpaths interlinking with these in a devilishly complex web. The deep cloughs were host to countless mills; old leats, ponds and ruins abound but few remain working today.

The most inspiring remains, however, are the trackbeds of the old tramways and ephemeral railways that served the quarries together with the slab-paved roadways which once saw horse drawn waggons or sleds transporting heroic-sized lumps of rock to the cutting and dressing shops and to the valley below. The best time to visit the tops is on a crisp, bright winters day, frost decorating the sedges and mosses and with the low sun and a dusting of snow picking out these man-made artefacts to a tee.

The Walk

Leave the Buck and walk downhill to the end of the terrace, then branch left and walk along in front of Brookland Terrace. At the far end of this turn left and walk up the rough road between the green garages, starting a steep climb up the side of the valley. Remain with this road and wind round to reach the house at the top. Go through the gate to the right of this renovated house and barn and immediately look for the stone trough to the right, beside which is a stile you should climb. Once over it stick with the field boundary on your left and walk up through the rough pastures, crossing stiles as and when necessary.

Pass by the fence made largely of corrugated iron sheeting and continue straight up the hillside to the moorland track, turning right along this. Ahead of you the flat topped hill is Cowpe Lowe, to your right a wide prospect over the Rossendale Valley to Bacup and, beyond here, the high moorlands on the West Yorkshire boundary, the edge of Brontë country. Walk on around the end of the hill, Black Hill, passing a deep, sharp cleft cut into the side of Cowpe Lowe on your right. Cross the stile to the left of the gate, walk straight across the track which is evidently heavily used by scrambling bikes and then bear half right, aiming for the gap in the embankment ahead. This embankment is the line of one of the old tramways which led from Cragg Quarry; your route lies along it so when you get to the gap scramble up onto the bank and walk with it off to the right along and around the southern flank of Cowpe Lowe.

Remain with this tramway for about a quarter of a mile; it eventually merges with the line of an old cartway across the moor, the rutted and worn slabs still standing proud along the route. Views ahead extend to Peels Monument above Ramsbottom. At the point where a deep walled trench appears on your left you should bear left over the short bank across this and then walk along the track known as Sand Beds Lane. Glimpses down into the Irwell Valley are allowed here, the large cream area on the far hillside to your right is an artificial ski slope above

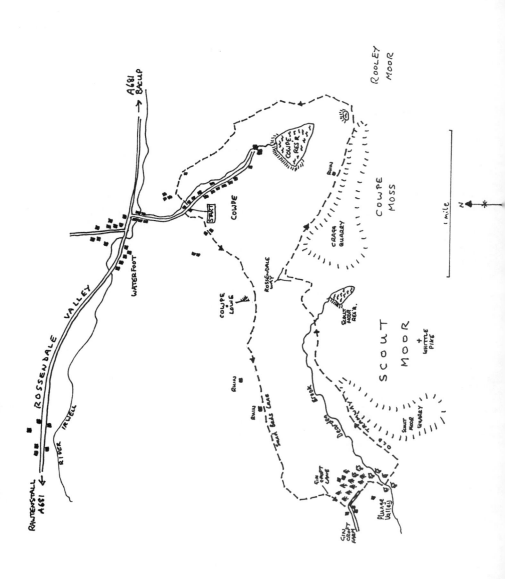

Rawtenstall. Cross the high stile when you reach it and remain with Sand Beds Lane. Several ruined farms are passed including the eponymous Sand Beds; it is impossible to imagine what life was like for the Victorian farmer in this wild, inhospitable place.

At the gate climb the ladder stile and walk along the track between the high banks, turning left at the end down the slightly better-surfaced Gin Croft Lane. Walk down this to the junction at the end of the woods and just above Gin Croft Farm. Turn left along the tarmac road at this point and walk along, continuing straight ahead as the tarred road swings left and wind down with this increasingly sunken pathway to reach the stream at the bottom, an area known as Plunge Valley. An information board here outlines the history of the area and the fulling mill, the remains of which are a few yards downstream.

Spend a little time exploring this site before crossing the footbridge across Dearden Brook and climbing the stile, then to walk ahead up the hillside past the lone ash tree. Once at the valley crest aim to walk ahead to pass the left end of the truncated wall and, from here, to the corner of the walls pointing towards you from higher up the hillside. At this corner is a small wooden gateway giving access to the sedge covered track on the far side. This is the line of an old tramway descending from the quarries high up the valley and you remain with the line of this for the next mile or so. The route is obvious if boggy in places but on occasion the trackbed disappears completely; simply sight it ahead and remain on the line. Old wooden sleepers remain in situ and at one point the track is still there showing the gauge to have been about 3'6". Down to your left the Dearden Brook has cut a glorious winding clough deep into the edge of Scout Moor. You'll have to cross several side cloughs, marked by waterfalls and on one occasion a rickety old sleeper bridge – cross just upstream as it is very slippery and precarious.

Pass through the gap in the wall marked by two old wooden gateposts and walk ahead around the hillside track, the dam of Scout Moor Reservoir coming into view ahead. Look down left into the clough to find the circular drain issuing from the hillside, just below the second cloughside wall up this deep side valley. Walk down the steep clough side to this drain and then up the equally steep far side, following the line of the wall. At the top you'll come to a concreted road, a service road for the reservoir. Turn left along this, go around the hairpin bend and walk along for a further hundred yards or so, then cut left up alongside the fin-like section of wall that marks the near hillside. Walk along this, and the line of wall beyond, up the hillside to regain the concrete road again, turning left along this.

At the point where this roadway sweeps off and down to the left look for the Rossendale Way (RW) waymark on the post to your right and go along the track here, the wall on your left. In a short distance turn right up the track and swing right with this at the ridge top, walking up towards the old quarry workings. Keep the wall close to your left, drifting away with this as it diverges left away from the main track. It's a rather melancholy landscape hereabouts, with overgrown spoil tips, chasms, sheep tracks and clumps of bilberry replacing the once thriving quarry workings here on Cowpe Moss.

Stick with the line of the wall going slowly downhill. Down on your left is the stretched polygonal lake of Cowpe Reservoir, below this is the mill at the head of Cowpe Village. Go through the rusty old gate by the standing stones and walk along to the ruin, after which the track gradually regains height. Pass through the gate you reach and walk ahead, again with the wall on your left. Cross above the small header reservoir – Cragg High Level Tank – and join the track that comes down from the right. In a hundred yards or so go left at the fork and walk downhill with the descending track, remaining with this past several water board signs to the point where it joins a further track coming down from the right; on the left is a small walled quarry with a pool filling its deepest recesses.

This new track, along which you turn left, is Rooley Moor Road, an old coach road between Rochdale and Rawtenstall. Until at least the 1920's an old coaching inn, The Moorcock, remained open about a mile to the south (behind you) on this bleak road. Walk downhill until you reach a gate across the road, at which point turn left and walk down alongside the brook to the gate. Go through the narrow kissing gate to the right of this and turn right, following the line of wall and ignoring the further stile on the right in a matter of a few yards. At the end of the field go through the gate and over the stile and walk down to the isolated cottage. Pass immediately to the right of the cottage and then walk along the fence away from it to the gate at the end. From here head for the black painted end gable of the terrace ahead. Cross the double stile before you reach this terrace and walk down the line of the vaccary slab fence, heading for the Buck which you can see in the valley below.

Vaccary Fencing, Cowpe

21. ROSSENDALE: NANGREAVES

Route: Nangreaves – Walmersley – Deeply Vale – Harden Moor – Grants Tower

Distance: 7.5 Miles

Map: Sheet SD 81/91 Bury, Rochdale and Littleborough

Start: The Lord Raglan, Nangreaves, Bury

Access: Travel north from Bury along the A56 for about two miles. On reaching the traffic lights at Walmersley Post Office (on your right) turn right up Old Road and follow it to its end, crossing over the M66 en route. Nangreaves and the Lord Raglan are both signposted from Old Road; the last half mile is cobbled.

The Lord Raglan (061 764 6680)

At the top end of the hamlet of Nangreaves, the Lord Raglan is in an enviable position on the lip of one of the ridges of high moorland which reach like the fingers of a giant hand down towards Manchester. Sitting on the terrace and supping some of the excellently kept Theakstons Best Bitter, Old Peculiar or Youngers No. 3, the immense view to the west encompasses the famous Peel's Tower on Holcombe (Harcles) Hill and the distant Winter Hill above Bolton, topped by its giant transmitter masts. Despite its proximity the M66 motorway is well screened; you're much more likely to hear the throaty cough of a steam locomotive on the East Lancashire Railway, far below, as it threads its way along the Irwell valley between Bury and Rawtenstall.

The pub is named in honour of Lord Raglan, overall commander of the British forces in the Crimean War. A clipping from the Bury Times, displayed at one end of the bar, records the death of this military man in 1855. The pub itself is somewhat older, being nearer two hundred years old. Until the turn of this century it also acted as the village butchers shop and greengrocers and had its own brewhouse, the latter now being incorporated into the fabric of this large, comfortable building. The current landlord, Brendan Leyden, was born in the pub; the latest of several generations to run the business he's always on the lookout for antiques to add to the already impressive collection on display in the multi-roomed pub.

A restaurant is an integral part of the pub offering a good choice of home cooked dishes including Worcestershire Trout. Those with less capacious appetites can choose from a wide variety of bar snacks and there's always at least one vegetarian choice on the menu. Children are welcome and muddy boots are a regular part of the scenery in this well run and welcoming pub. The Lord Raglan is open daily from noon to 3 pm (last food 2 pm) and 7 pm to 11 pm (last food 10-ish).

Nangreaves

Apart from a few isolated farmsteads Nangreaves did not exist until the end of the Eighteenth century when John Hall built a mill high on this hillside to the east of Ramsbottom. From 1803 until the 1960's the mill workers produced high quality cotton goods. They were housed in solid gritstone terraces adjoining the mill and enclosing the mill yard and mill pond. The decline of the cotton industry in the 1960's led to the replacement of cotton as the product by polystyrene goods and this business survived until the mid 1980's when the mill was finally closed. Very recently the low mill buildings have been adapted and converted into cottages and the mill yard and pond have become a village green. The whole is now a conservation area; it is doubtful whether contemporary mill workers could afford to live in Nangreaves today.

To the north of the hamlet are the scant remains of Grants Tower. This was built in 1829 for William and Daniel Grant who first developed the calico printing industry in nearby Ramsbottom and became great benefactors to the area. It is believed that Charles Dickens modelled the Cheeryble Brothers, in Nicholas Nickleby, on the Grants. A walking guide from the 1920's records that the key to the Tower was held at the nearby farm and that panoramic views were available from the top. Sadly only the barest of skeletons of this old tower now survives.

The Cheesden Valley

Long before the towns of south Lancashire became famous for their textile and cotton industries this tiny Pennine valley was a hive of activity, host to a dozen or more mills, dyeing and print works. They developed here to take advantage of the abundant clean water supply, local wool and emergent coal seams; only later did they partially adapt to and utilize the cheap imported cotton which eventually saw the rise of

the familiar cotton towns and the decline of the industry in Cheesden –
only one bleach works now remains operational, some miles downstream from this walk. The most extensive remains are those at Deeply
Vale Print Works where cobbled lanes, bridges, conduits and wheel pits
remain below the dam of the mill reservoir. The most spectacular
remains, however, are at the very head of the valley where the facade of
the Cheesden Lumb Woollen Mill all but fills the valley, brooding over
the tumbled remains of countless buildings and mill lodges (ponds). The
whole valley and tributaries have been recognised as a site of major
historic significance by English Heritage and are under its protection.

The Walk

Turn left from the pub and walk uphill. In about fifty yards you'll find
some stone steps set into the wall on your right, before you get to the
farm. Climb these into the field and follow the path uphill to a stile in
the corner. This short climb has opened up extensive views to the south
over the Greater Manchester conurbation – city centre Manchester is
easily picked out by its concentration of tall buildings – and to the
Mersey estuary and the Cheshire Plain. The walk now gently descends
this southern slope of Snape Hill; head towards Whitewall Farm,
crossing another stone stile in the first wall you reach and then aiming
for a stile directly behind the electricity pylon, about thirty yards to the
right of the farm. Cross directly over the drive here and enter the field
opposite, cross a further stile to the right of the small area of trees ahead
and walk down to the minor road.

On reaching this road, a driveway, turn sharp left and walk down to the
ivy clad cottage. A yellow waymarker points the way from here which is
down the walled path in front of the cottage and, having crossed the
stile at the end, bear right. You're now in a beautiful secluded valley,
well wooded with alder, sycamore, willow, thorn and oak and dotted
with a string of small ponds which, long ago, provided power to the
long-gone mill further down the valley. Keep half an eye out here for
heron, coot, moorhen and the vivid flash of a kingfisher. Cross the
footbridge which forms part of one of the dam walls and scramble up
the bank opposite, climbing the steep stile at the top to gain a narrow
road, turning right down this. The steep bank to your left is thickly clad
with bilberry plants and heather, a sure sign of approaching moorland.
Ahead the M66 strides across the small valley en route from Bury to
Rawtenstall whilst on your right is a flat, scrubby area and a couple of
gateposts, all that remain of the mill once fed from the ponds upstream.

Before reaching the motorway bridge the way is left, up along White Carr Lane and towards Walmersley Golf Course. Bear left again and follow this road for nearly a mile. The only building you pass is White Carr Farm, an old, low gritstone building with glorious mullioned windows. Not far past this, around the sharp bends, is a board

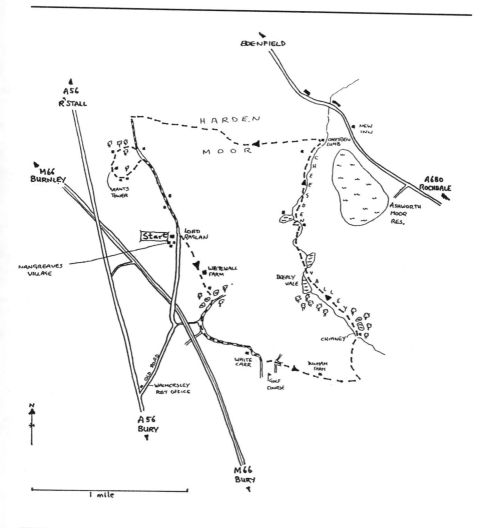

welcoming you to Walmersley Golf Course, stretching away from you along the hillside. At this point take the stile on your left and follow the wall up the hillside, bearing right at the top to reach a gate and a signpost. Of the three possible ways you want the middle one, signposted to Birtle Dean. This is known as Scotland Lane, a long established moorland road still, in places, surfaced with setts. Follow this road through the isolated farmyard of Dunham Farm and continue along the hillside, the deep trough of Cheesden Brook emerging ahead, the flat-topped Knowle Hill dominating the horizon.

Cross between the old stone gateposts and follow the track around the hillside for about fifty yards until a vista of the deep valley opens before you. Pause here to appreciate the view across Rochdale in the middle distance to the heights of the South Pennines at Saddleworth Moor, marked by a radio mast which also marks the route of the Pennine Way National Footpath. Down and off to your left an old chimneystack rises above the trees which cover the floor of the Cheesden Valley here, this chimney is our next target.

Turn back-left on yourself and follow the path down the steep valley side, crossing the stile at the bottom and winding across an area of old coal workings, heading always for the old chimney stack. Cross the brook by the old single arched pack horse bridge and turn left up the valley. The chimney marks the site of the old Lower Wheel Print Works, other remains include piles of dressed stone in the swiftly flowing, crystal clear brook and some mill lodges behind the chimney. These are home, in season, to an abundance of dragonfly and damselfly, frogs, heron and various species of duck. The valley is rich, too, in mammal life, fox, rabbit, stoat, weasel and white hares can all be seen. Follow the path away from the old works and up the hillside, turning left where it joins a wider track and walk up to the woods on your left. These hide the remains of Deeply Vale Print Works, well worth exploring in detail if with a little caution.

Pass the lake on your left, at the end of which is a small quarry from where the stone to build the mills and construct the dams emanated. Continue along the track, another lake appearing to your right. At the top of the slope look ahead for the squat pylon and, beyond this, a cottage next to a waterfall. Head across the fields towards this cottage, turn left along its drive and walk along for about a hundred yards, passing a large barn on your right built on the remains of Longland Cotton Mill. Once past the barn turn back-right on yourself and walk along the top of the dam. The old Buckhurst school looms over the far bank of the lake whilst beyond is the edifice of Peel's Tower. Pass through the gateposts at the end of the dam and then turn left by the telegraph pole, walk down to the stream side and follow this upstream. The way is rather indistinct for the next half mile or so and can be quite marshy beneath the veneer of sedges, reeds and mosses. Aim for the stile by the white-painted "sheep grazing" sign and work your way from here to the left of the valley floor.

Continue up the valley passing by and through overgrown old buildings and drained lodges until you reach the facade of Cheesden Lumb Woollen Mill, the last works in the valley; its splendour has recently been tempered by storm damage although work is in hand to restore this. The crenellated wall on the valley crest to the right marks the dam wall of Ashworth Moor Reservoir. The isolated white building at the head of the side valley ahead is the New Inn, a Bass pub which also does snacks for those who need sustenance at this stage of the walk.

From the woollen mill turn left immediately this side of the footbridge, pass through the stile and turn left, walking up the short moorland track to a driveway. Go straight across this and enter the field to the left of the wall, following the wall up and onto Harden Moor. The right of way across the moors here is undefined, the simplest way of remaining on course is to aim straight for Peel's Tower, visible in the middle distance. After about a mile and a half bear slightly right to head for the light coloured waste tip that marks the edge of an old quarry. Pass over several broken walls to reach the base of the spoil heap at a gate, leave the field here and turn left along Bury Old Road, an unmade, walled, moorland track. Up to the right a large circle of stones marks the site of an old cairn on the nearby hilltop.

Take the second turn on the right, a road signposted to Hillside Kennels and graced by a sign-board in the likeness of Peter Pan. Follow the road round through the trees and into the yard of Pike Farm, then turn left and walk up the road to the small transmission station near the hilltop, passing to the right of this. Immediately beyond is the stump that is all that remains of Grants Tower; its height or view from the top can only be imagined. Follow the path around the south side of the hill (ie the opposite side to that which you approached it from) and walk down to the left hand farm in the lee of the slope. Turn left here at the iron gates and follow this driveway back along to Bury Old Road, turning right along here to return to the Lord Raglan about half a mile away.

22. ROSSENDALE: MERECLOUGH

Route: Mereclough – Hurstwood – Swinden Valley – Worsthorne – Hurstwood

Distance: 7 Miles

Map: O.S Outdoor Leisure series Sheet 19 South Pennines

Start: The Kettledrum Inn, Mereclough, Burnley

Access: The Kettledrum Inn stands beside a minor road leading from Burnley to Hebden Bridge just over two miles south-east of Burnley. From Burnley take the A671 road past the entrance to Towneley Hall and Park and then turn onto the A646 towards Holme Chapel and Todmorden. Cross under the railway line and, on entering the hamlet of Walk Mill, turn sharp left along Park Road. After a few yards hairpin to the right and follow the road up to the T-junction in Over Town. Turn left here and remain with this road to reach Mereclough in about half a mile. The Kettledrum is the second pub on the right.

The Kettledrum Inn (0282 24591)

I've been to umpteen pubs in my time (all in the cause of professional research of course) but only one (the incredible Yew Tree at Cauldon, near Leek, Staffordshire) can beat the extraordinary collection of artefacts and brasses that Roy and Pauline Ratcliffe have amassed in their twenty-odd years in the licensed trade, the last ten years of which have been spent building up the Kettledrum from near dereliction. It's worth making the trip simply for the view from the pub, high on a ridge overlooking Burnley far below and across to Pendle Hill and the high fells of the Forest of Bowland in north Lancashire. Inside, the pub is an Alladins cave, every square foot of available wall, beam or floor space is taken with brass and copper plates, weights, measures, bedpans, gauges, oil lamp bases and brass trays from long-defunct breweries. What doesn't gleam can be buffed or polished – Toby jugs, walking sticks, spears, swords, cutlasses and daggers with and without scabbards, boomerangs and hurling sticks, shuttles and shillelagh. There's a fine display of old photographs – note the one of the pub in the late 1970's to see how much work the current owners have put in – whilst upstairs in the gas-lit restaurant is an Indenture document, a deed of sale from 1825 recording the transfer of the property to a schoolmaster.

The Kettledrum Inn, Mereclough

It was not until 1861 that the building became a pub, named after the Derby winner of that year which was owned by the Towneley family, Lords of the Manor, whose stately home is now a museum outside Burnley. The year 1861 marked an upturn in their fortunes; since then family members (including a current one) have often been High Sheriff of Lancashire. The pub once belonged to a local brewery, Masseys of Burnley, now long defunct. Nowadays it is a free house selling the full range of Theakstons (Best Bitter, XB and Old Peculier), Courage Directors and John Smiths Magnet Best Bitter, all served by handpump at the – you've guessed it – sheet-coppered bar.

Also available is a very extensive range of bar meals including a vegetarian selection so vast that you should go there the day before to start reading. Food is available from 12 to 3 and 6 to 11, the pub itself is open from 11 am to 3 pm and 5.30 pm to 11 pm. Local ramblers often frequent this ideally situated pub and local walking/history guides can be purchased along with your next pint.

The Walk

Leave the pub and turn left down the minor road which runs down beside it, signposted for Heptonstall and Blackshawhead; both these are in West Yorkshire, the pub is only a couple of miles from the County boundary. Wind round with the road, remaining with the main drag and

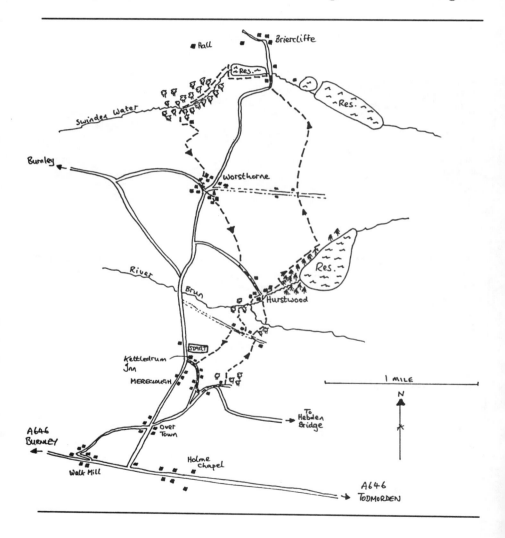

climb the steep, winding hill out of the clough, passing the small huddles of Eighteenth century – and earlier – cottages. Round the bend at the top of the slope and look for the public footpath sign on the left, pointing along the driveway to Drakeshead Kennels and Cattery.

Follow this driveway for about a hundred yards, passing a house and garden on your left, then look carefully for the stone steps set into the high wall on your left. Climb these and then follow the narrow path between spinney and covered reservoir and climb the wall at the end. Just ahead, next to the gate, a further stile marked with two waymark arrows gives access to the field. Once in the field bear half right, looking to the wall on the near horizon for a narrow gap stile, just to the right of the straggly line of trees. Pass through this gap stile and walk straight ahead. The next stile is in the wall ahead about ten yards to the right of the dilapidated field gate. Once over this head half left across the rough pasture heading for the gap in the fence marked by two concrete posts. From here descend the slope heading for the bottom corner of the fir tree plantation on your left; upon reaching this walk downhill for a few yards to leave the field via a small wooden gate in the corner and turn left along the drive.

Within fifty yards look for the stile to the right, immediately before the small bungalow's garden and by the lone telegraph pole. Cross this stile, the footbridge beyond and then the waymarked stile, then walk down the steep slope beyond, keeping to the left of the trees where possible to reach a stream at the bottom. Cross the wooden footbridge beyond yet another stile and turn left, following the path gently up the valley side to join a wider track, going ahead along this. Cross a further stile then another stream and bear left, walking along to reach the hamlet of Hurstwood.

This tiny hamlet retains its old manor house, Hurstwood Hall (built by Barnard Towneley in 1576 for his new bride, Agnes Ormerod, who was all of ten years old) and the adjoining Manor Farm together with a huddle of mullion windowed ivy covered cottages and houses. One of these, Spensers House, is reputed to have been home for a while to the Elizabethan poet Edmund Spenser, contemporary of Shakespeare and author of classic poems such as The Faerie Queene and The Shepheardes Calender. Another famous resident, this time at the farm, was Richard Tattersall, founder of the horse sales which bear his name. What you miss here on this outward leg you can see on the return journey.

Turn right at the telephone box and walk along the rough road, the Baptist Chapel standing proud to your left followed by a terrace of gritstone houses and an old farm. Just past the farm cross the stile and walk up the wide, green, walled path. At the end of the wall bear left and follow the obvious path up out of the valley, largely filled by the fir tree plantation that is now Hurstwood. Go through the metal kissing gate at the top and join the steep path that skirts the edge of the wood. Simply remain with this path, climbing steps and crossing stiles as necessary; glimpses of Hurstwood Reservoir may be had down through the trees on your right.

Cross the stile at the end of the first tract of woodland and, where the waymarkers indicate a split in the path, turn left, following initially a wall on your left and then an obvious path across the moorland pasture. Follow this path across several fields, crossing stiles as appropriate and aim for the right hand corner of the long, low garage which is the nearest building to you. To the left are extensive views over Burnley to Pendle Hill, further to the right Kelbrook Moor and in the distance the southernmost hills of the Yorkshire Dales above Skipton.

Cross the moorland track immediately above the garage and follow the cindered track which leads away beyond it, gaining access to this via two stiles. Stick with this track for the next half mile or so. The hilltop to your right, Wasnop Edge, has an ancient tumulus and a cairn circle on its crest; to your left beyond the small dump, marked by telegraph poles, is the site of a stone circle but there's hardly anything left to see. You'll get to a field gate, to the left of which is a kissing gate made from an old door; go through the kissing gate and walk on with the fence on your right. Eventually the field boundaries funnel in from either side; cross the stile at the far left hand corner of this funnel and then walk around to the left with the path, keeping the wall to your left. The two reservoirs below are the Swinden Reservoirs, ahead the tiny settlement of Briercliffe. Gradually work down to the field track and follow this to its end, joining the minor road and walking downhill to the bridge.

Turn left immediately before this bridge, pass through the kissing gate and walk along the track alongside the reservoir wall. Up to your right the multi-windowed building on the hillcrest is the Roggerham Gate Inn (Youngers Ales, bar snacks); virtually straight ahead on the hillside the sombre gritstone edifice is Extwistle Hall. This medieval building was left virtually as a shell by a gunpowder explosion in 1717; used intermittently since then as a barn, cattle house and accommodation it is currently being restored but is not open to the public.

Follow the path across the dam, climb the tall stone step stile at the end and turn left, following the path to, alongside and eventually into the broadleaf woodlands, always remaining to the right of the stream. The clough becomes fairly steep sided, the path in parts flagged with gritstone blocs. On reaching the wooden post marked with red arrows go to the left, work down to the stream and cross it on the stepping stones, climbing the steps up the steep valleyside opposite to the pasture at the top. Walk straight ahead to another guidepost, this one with yellow arrows, and turn left, cross the stile and walk on to the drive in front of Wood Hey Farm. Walk along this drive around the double bend and to its end at the playing fields at Worsthorne. At the new changing room block turn right and walk along the rough road in front of the terrace. This is Lennox Street; walk along to its end and bear left (not down Gordon Street), remaining with this main village street to reach the village green.

The village of Worsthorne has been much extended but the green remains intact, bordered by church, inn, school and old cottages. You should head half left to walk between the church on your left and the Bay Horse (Bass Beers) to your right, then turning right along Green Terrace. Walk to the end then bear left at the two garages and walk along the paved path, a brook to your left, a walled garden on your right. Wind along to the end, go through the kissing gate and into the field. The paved path continues, intermittently, across the field, simply follow it across several fields to emerge on a minor road and turn left along this back down into Hurstwood.

At the hamlet centre turn right in front of the Hall and walk towards the farmyard, but turn left before you reach the first cottage and descend the path into the wooded clough. In this wooded clough it is believed that the Tenth Century Battle of Brunenburk was fought. Cross the substantial stone footbridge over the river Brun and follow the track, then path, left as it winds up the other side. This becomes a walled footpath, emerging eventually into the edge of a farmyard and in front of the white-painted Rose Cottage. Walk to the left of the hedge, up past the cottage to the farm drive. To the left at the isolated bungalow is a small wildlife sanctuary; you should turn right, walk through the area of farmyard buildings and along the drive beyond.

Pass a large house on your right and soon reach a hanger of Beech trees, also on the right. Opposite this is a stone stile into the field (if you're doing this walk on April 1st then continue along to the end of this drive and turn left to return to the pub, the reason for this follows). Go over this stile and follow the well used path down the dry valley, crossing a further stile on your right a short while later. Continue along the path to reach a small stile which takes you into the back garden of Mereclough House, passing then between this and a cottage. Looking to your right at the side wall of the house you'll see a notice proclaiming "No public right of way. Permitted footpath only. Closed every April 1st for 24 hours. Highways Act, 1980, Section 31." This essentially allows the public to use the footpath but without it becoming a dedicated right of way. Such exist in many parts of the country; one in Derbyshire charges one penny for the right of passage on the same date each year. On reaching the road beyond turn right uphill to reach the Kettledrum again.

23. NORTH LUNE: HORNBY

Route: Hornby – Loyn Bridge – Arkholme – Gressingham – The Snab

Distance: 8 Miles

Map: Sheet 637 Burton-in Kendal and Caton

Start: The Royal Oak, Hornby

Access: Hornby is on the A683 Lancaster to Kirkby Lonsdale road about nine miles north east of Lancaster, seven miles north east of Junction 34 on the M6 (Lancaster North and Morecambe turn). The Royal Oak is on the left at the northern end of the village.

The Royal Oak (05242 21228)

This old, stone-built roadside inn is a listed building and dates from 1781, a stone plaque built into the front of the building records that it was built in that year for William and Emma Gelderd. Presumably they were also farmers as the pub was only half of the size it is today; a barn survived in use until after the second war when it was put to use as a cafe, eventually being incorporated into the pub-proper in the late 1960's when local Lancaster brewers Yates and Jackson took over from Bass. They largely gutted the old pub and generated their ideal of a comfortable village local, the results of which remain largely unchanged today. The brewery sold up in 1984; Thwaites of Blackburn took over many of their pubs including this one, where landlord Ian Fell keeps an exceptional pint of their award winning bitter.

The one roomed pub features a lot of exposed stonework, liberally dressed with brasses, plates, toby jugs and the occasional oddment or two – look for the enormous wooden pipe and the stuffed badger in the games room, not only head but front legs and torso leaping out over the pool table. This games area is largely separate from the main area which is laid out with "traditional" pub mocquette chairs and low tables together with a few wall seats and high-backed benches to one end. The Royal Oak is open from 11.30 to 3 and 6 to 11, bar meals are served between noon and 2 pm and 6 pm to 9 pm (on average...) and children are very welcome.

Hornby

Dominating the village is the extravagant castle, Victorian exuberance at its best (or worst), embattlements and turrets leap-frogging each other ever higher above the wooded slopes of the river Wenning; perhaps Disney once paid a call. The original Thirteenth Century Pele Tower is buried somewhere within the pile which originally was the home of the Stanley family. Sir Edward Stanley commanded a contingent of troops at the battle of Flodden Field (in Northumberland) in 1513, this victory over the Scots earned him the title Lord Monteagle. The Stanleys are long gone; the castle has passed through the hands of a string of owners and is a private residence not open to the public. It is best viewed either from the village's bridge or from the main road to the southwest, with a low evening sun highlighting the grey/red sandstone in which it is built.

The village itself is little more than a long main street leading to a bridge over the Wenning, the houses and cottages are largely Georgian in origin. The church of St. Margarets acted as the castle's chapel; it has a very rare octagonal tower built for Sir Edward as thanks for his deliverance from, and victory at, Flodden. The large drinking fountain at the road junction south of the river is dated 1858; the playful badge attached recalls a former owner of the castle, Pudsey Dawson, who introduced myriad cats into the castle, then uninhabited, to rid it of a plague of rats. Priory Farm, standing alone on its knoll above the Lune just west of the village, is the site of a medieval priory, the only remnant of which is part of a Saxon cross now housed in St. Margarets church.

Nearby Gressingham huddles in the narrow neck of Gressingham Beck. Many of the cottages date from Stuart times although the village is recorded in Domesday. The church originates from Saxon times and houses a cross dating from 850; the adjoining Hall dates from 1688, a squat three storey building with fine mullioned windows. The Beck winds down the centre of the hamlet in a deep, winding cleft.

NORTH LUNE

Using a geological generalisation the river Lune divides an outlying bloc of Mountain Limestone (more familiar as the dominant rock of the Yorkshire Dales) from the Gritstone massif of Bowland. North west of the river this area of Lancashire is characterised by typical limestone scenery, a craggy landscape bounded by extensive limestone "pavements" and with few surface streams. This geology results in a distinct flora, Ash woodlands predominate and the vivid green grass is rich with lime loving plants: Lily-of-the-Valley, Hawkbit and Knapweed for example. The buildings, too, have that characteristic, mellow, light colouring in contrast to the dour gritstone of much of the County; compare the villages north of Morecambe with those east of Preston, for example. The Lune itself is one of the cleanest rivers in Britain and has one of the best salmon runs; a weeks fishing can well cost four figures. The artist J.M.W. Turner was captivated by the river, one of his most famous landscapes was painted at the Crook of Lune, just east of Lancaster. To the west of this city the river sweeps into Morecambe Bay through some of the most extensive sandbanks and salt marshes in the country, to the north most of the coastline is either nature reserve or A.O.N.B.

The Walk

Walk up Hornby's one main street and at the junction at the top bear left towards Gressingham. Wind along and down this minor road for about half a mile to reach the narrow old Loyn Bridge across the Lune. Just before you bend round to this, a stile on your right leads to a path up to an old pill box in the field, behind which is the excellently preserved motte and bailey castle, Castle Stede. The motte, or mound, at the far end is now capped with trees and the bailey, or enclosure, is very well defined; you're on a public footpath so linger to appreciate the site.

Return to Loyn Bridge and cross it, walk along past the lay-by and enter the field on the right at the signpost to Thrushgill Wood and Arkholme. For the next two miles follow the Lune upstream, passing through Thrushgill Wood and several other copses and leaving the riverbank from time to time as the obvious line of path dictates your course. Views ahead and to the right are spectacular and remain with you throughout the walk. You get an unusual angle on Ingleborough, its sculptured northern face dominating the Pennine edge far behind the village of Melling. Peeking out behind and beyond this, the sharp edge of Pen-y-Ghent cuts the distant horizon whilst to the north the gentler rounded tops of Leck Fell (at just over 2000' the highest point in Lancashire) and the southern end of the Howgill Fells dominate the horizon.

You can see the village of Arkholme ahead of you on a low ridge above the river. Aim to pass to the right of the white house which stands at the foot of this ridge near the riverbank. Beyond this are two cottages; at the foot of their garden a stile leads past a field gate onto a track which

Hornby Castle and River Wenning

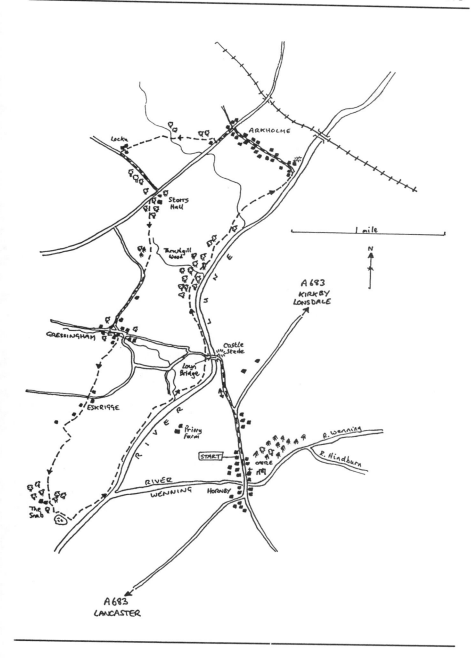

curves up to the left and becomes the one village street of Arkholme. First right off this street will take you to the tiny St. John's Chapel and beyond this the motte of an old castle; the views from the footpath here are excellent. Return to the village street and walk up it. The street is lined with myriad old cottages, barns and farmhouses, many with dates on their lintel or corbel stone going back to the early 1600's. At the top of the street turn left along the main road. The idyllic little Bay Horse pub on the corner opposite is sadly, despite the sign outside, one of only two Mitchell's pubs to serve keg beer.

Walk along the footpath to the second public footpath sign on the right. Turn right into the drive leading up to the farmyard, pass through the first gate about thirty yards along and look for the stile on your right. Cross this and skirt the farmyard, passing through the gap stile beside the gate at the far end. From here walk across the field heading for the left hand side of the line of trees at the far side. Go through the gate next to these trees and follow the track up the left hand side of the next field. Look for the footbridge on your left a couple of yards to the left of the wooden post which stands isolated towards the edge of the field. From the stile at the far end of the footbridge take a bearing on the roof of the house which pokes out above the near-hillside and walk up towards this. Go through the gate in the wire fence and then enter the small paddock beside the house. Leave this by the gate at the far side and walk up around the house, across the gritted yard in front of the cottages and to the minor road. Turn left along this and walk down to the main road.

On reaching the main road turn right and cross it. In the estate to the left is the gothic-style mansion of Storrs Hall; the cottage at the gatehouse has a datestone of 1743. Pass the entrance drive to the Hall and then go left through the green door in the wall at the public footpath sign. Walk along the short, railed section and climb the stile at the end. From here look half right to locate a stile in the wire fence, walk to and climb this and then aim for a second stile on the hill top about fifty yards to the left of the birch and fir plantation. Once over this veer slightly right to reach the field gate in the corner beside a small copse. Go over the stile beside this and walk left down the narrow road to the hamlet of Gressingham.

At the fork bear right and walk over the shoulder of the hill down to the T-junction. Cross virtually straight over here, going down the lane beside the telephone box to the series of railed paths and footbridges across the stream. Walk across these and up the path at the far side, turning left along the narrow road at the top. In less than a hundred yards look on the right for a yellow waymark arrow pointing up a drive guarded by an unusual wooden gate. Go up here, through the gate at the end and up the narrow paddock beyond, at the end of which is a stile in the left hand corner. Cross this and head for the oak tree in the top right corner of the field. Climb the stile beneath this and walk steeply uphill to the top right corner of this field, near which a further stile leads into a long paddock. At the far end of this cross through the wire fence (using the wire mesh gate) and walk to the field gate beyond. Once through this walk along the farm track to the minor road.

This is the scattered community of Eskrigge. Go straight across the road and along the track opposite. Walk in front of the rebuilt cottages and through the gate beyond, sticking to the right hand boundary and passing the barn conversion. At the end of the field climb the fence stile and bear right to the stone gateposts. Go left up the old lane here and in a matter of yards fork left beneath the holly trees. Walk up this sunken lane to the top and bear right along the line of fence, keeping it on your left for about a hundred yards. At the rusty field gate that you meet head-on at the offset field corner enter the field the gate leads into, follow the hedge to the hilltop and then down the other side. Down to your left is the gravelly confluence of the Wenning with the Lune.

On reaching the field corner by the large oak tree pass through the gate and bear half left down the field towards the fence to the left of the barn. Cross the stile at your end of this fence and then walk along the edge of the woods, passing to the left of the barn. Go through the gate at the end and turn left, following the rough, then surfaced drive leading away from the house called The Snab. After about a hundred yards go through the gate on your left, marked with a waymark arrow. Walk down the slope and then turn right, passing the large pond to your right which is well populated with swans, Canada and Pink-footed Geese and duck. You're heading for the riverbank about fifty yards to the right of the isolated hut. Cross the stile here and then walk upstream. From here simply follow the riverside path, diverging with it as necessary to reach Loyn Bridge some distance upstream; crossing the bridge to return to Hornby.

24. NORTH LUNE: OVERTON

Route: Overton – Bazil Point – Sunderland Point – Potts Corner

Distance: 6.5 Miles

Map: Sheet SD 45/55 Galgate and Dolphinholme

Start: The Ship Hotel, Overton, near Lancaster

Access: From Lancaster take the A589 towards Morecambe and turn off at the new roundabout along the B5273 towards Heysham. At the mini-roundabout take the exit signposted to Middleton and Overton (N.B. this is a tide-affected road). Pass the Golden Ball pub and continue along this tidal road, turning left just before the line of pylons crosses the road to reach Overton. The pub is beside the village's main street. If the road is flooded by the tide then return to the B5273 and drive through to Heysham, following the signs for the docks. Just before the docks, where the main road bends sharp right at traffic lights, continue straight ahead to Middleton and thence Overton.

The Ship Hotel (052471 231)

The Ship is rather akin to Dr. Who's Tardis: a time capsule containing a lot more than would seem possible at a cursory glance from outside. Apart from the cigarette and fruit machines (and the modest price of the beer) time stopped late last century. A glorious Victorian polished wood bar, complete with glass architraves, remains the focal point, bedecked with a range of handpumps offering Daniel Thwaites's Mild and Bitter. To discover the pub's hidden depths, however, climb the steps beside the bar and venture a look into the snug or back room. Here you'll find an incredible collection of birds eggs and stuffed birds. These pastimes were common amongst the Victorian gentry and the collection amassed at The Ship must be typical of such; I doubt, however, whether the display in the snug can have a rival anywhere.

The rest of the furnishings reflect the Victorian era, comfortable settees, old solid chairs and tables, long-case clocks and a muted collection of brasses and pictures. The current licensees, Yvonne and Kevin Bromley, have been at The Ship for only a few short years, coming in soon after

Thwaites took over the pub from the defunct Lancaster brewers, Yates and Jackson. They've got a hard act to follow in the shape of Ma Mcklusky. This formidable lady was licensee for over fifty years earlier this century. Her word was law; her reputation at dealing with drunks – ejecting brawling sailors two at a time for example – legendary. The pub was known locally as Ma Mcklusky's, her Edwardian principles well respected by (almost) all who used the pub. The Bromleys are, thankfully, somewhat less bellicose and extend a warm and friendly welcome to all-comers. From Wednesday to Sunday a full bar meals service is provided, all home prepared and cooked; on Mondays and Tuesdays sandwiches are available – Yvonne will even pack them for you to take on your walk. The pub is open from 11.30 am to 3.30 pm (ish) and from 7 pm to 11 pm.

Sunderland Point

The river Lune empties into Morecambe Bay a few miles south west of Lancaster. Along the western side of the estuary a narrow spit of land has, over the centuries, survived the combined erosive efforts of the river and the sea. Rising a matter of but a few feet above the surrounding salt marshes, this is the Sunderland promontory.

Like its more famous namesake in the north east, Sunderland was once an important port. Unlike its namesake, however, the lifeblood of Lancashire's Sunderland was not shipbuilding but more general cargoes and with more than a passing interest in the slave trade. Whether slaves were ever actually incarcerated in the small warehouses, some of which survive as private dwellings, as some commentators have suggested is a moot point. Certainly Sunderland benefited indirectly from slavery; it is claimed that the first bales of American cotton to reach these Islands were shipped through the port. An old house on the promontory is named Cotton Tree House, the large tree growing by its front door is said to be a cotton tree, germinated from a seed which fell from one of these bales (I've also seen it described as a Black Oak, a Black Poplar and a Kapok). Other cargoes included hardwood, molasses, tobacco and gunpowder.

Established by the Quaker merchant Robert Lawson, Sunderland acted as the port for Lancaster and was busy as such by the early 1700's; seagoing vessels preferred the moorings of Sunderland to the tortuous and treacherous approach up the Lune to Lancaster. Cargoes were offloaded and stored at Sunderland before continuing overland or by lighter to the old County town. Fortunes were made by merchants based at Sunderland at the expense of those trading from Lancaster; this led to the development of the rival Glasson Dock in the early 1800's which in turn resulted in the very rapid decline of Sunderland, virtually all its trade was lost and only a few fishing smacks remained.

Today it is difficult to imagine Sunderland as a busy port. The moorings have gone, the channel is largely silted up; warehouses, stores and the tavern are now private houses or have disappeared completely. What remains is a strand of cottages and houses along a sandy road on the leeward side of the promontory cut off at high tide from the rest of Lancashire when the narrow road through the marshes is underwater. Even the post box is emptied only when tidal conditions allow. A few yachts and fishing cobles still use the foreshore as a base but essentially the hamlet is now a quiet backwater on the lonely, windswept promontory, a seventh heaven for birdwatchers and those seeking a day completely away from it all.

The Walk

Walk uphill from the pub for a few yards and turn left along Chapel View. Pass by the renovated barn on your right and turn right up the footpath signposted for Hall Greaves and Chapel Lane, then keeping left at each opportunity to emerge eventually on a surfaced road. Turn right down this and, at the junction by the post box, go straight ahead. Keep left at the fork, pass the houses to your right and walk along the track across the field, crossing a cattle grid to reach the front of a pebble-dashed cottage.

At this point look to your left to find the public footpath which descends the steps and goes along the foreshore, soon passing below a further cottage. From here there are excellent views across the estuary to Glasson Dock. Simply follow the shoreline around to reach Bazil Point; you can see the shipping channel marked out from Glasson whilst the houses across the water ahead are at Sunderland. Remain on the foreshore and turn your back on the estuary, walking now along the edge of the salt marsh to your left; there are public footpaths both on the land side and marsh side of the fence, the choice is yours as they both end up at the same spot, a white ladder stile leading onto a path which goes up over the hill and back to Overton. You, however, should not climb this stile but instead remain beside the marsh, picking your way along to the surfaced road a few hundred yards further on. On reaching this road you have a choice. If the tide is on its way out or is at low water then you can simply turn left here and walk along the road across

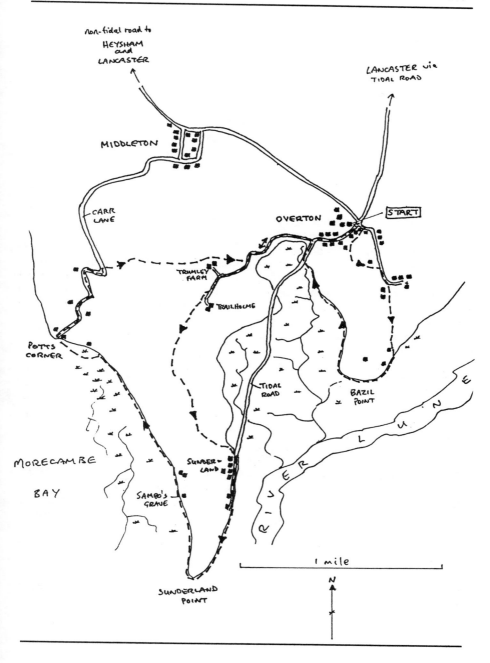

the marshes to Sunderland. If, however, the tide is on its way in or fully up then this road will be flooded. In this case turn right and walk up over the bank to the junction.

Turn left at this junction along the road signposted "cul de sac" and follow it, bearing left at every opportunity. You'll end up walking along a concrete-surfaced farm drive towards Trailholme – look for the small white guidepost. Walk along this drive, ignoring the public footpath sign on your right after just a few paces. About twenty yards before the track swings left to approach the farm is a stile through the hedge on your right. Go over this, turn left and follow the field boundary along two fields. At the end of the second field go through the gate and turn right, walking along the slab-surfaced path alongside the barbed wire fence. At the end cross the small stile on your left and walk along the bank to the white ladder stile. Once over this look to the diagonally opposite corner of the field (virtually straight ahead of you), walk to and climb the further white ladder stile there. From here walk half left across the field to the footbridge in the far-left corner. Cross it (mind the cross-bolts, presumably there to stop agile animals from crossing) and then remain with the field drain, crossing a further two bridges. The subsequent bridge you'll reach is derelict, the ditch having been filled in. From this spot head half left to the fence across the levee (bank), then climb the sets of steps to access the foreshore and walk along to Sunderland.

Remain with the road (which is a public footpath) and walk along past the strand of cottages and houses, passing the Cotton Tree and, eventually, the Old Hall. Beyond the Old Hall walk along the concreted edge of the green to gain access to the foreshore (the area between high tide mark and low tide mark is public domain) and walk along the pebbly beach to the end of the promontory at Sunderland Point.

The prospect from the Point is both diverse and extensive. Straight ahead is the Wyre, the tall chimney marks the I.C.I. works at Fleetwood. Nearer to hand the lighthouse is Plover Scar Light, marking the shipping channel up to Glasson and Lancaster; the squat, slightly askew building on the shore near this is the Chapter House of Cockersand Abbey. To your left the line of the Forest of Bowland dominates the horizon; the white buildings on the hillside nearer to hand are Lancaster University. To the north of these you can pick out the domed Ashton Memorial in Lancaster. Close at hand the estuary teems with wildfowl of every shape, size and colour; tiny Knot to large Heron, colourful and noisy Oystercatcher and Shellduck, silent and deadly Little Owl and Hawks.

Continue on round the Point and walk northwards along the shoreline. Ahead is the reactor of Heysham Power Station, beyond which the mountains of southern Lakeland form a spectacular skyline. The ferries you may see operate year-round to the Isle of Man whilst far out to sea the keen-eyed should pick out some of the gas rigs on the Morecambe Bay natural gas field. Several minutes walk will bring you to the enclosure, on your right, of Sambo's Grave, a small white cross and a poignant epitaph stamped on a brass plaque marking the site of the grave of this unfortunate African servant. He died here at the Brewhouse in Sunderland after his master left him here whilst he himself went away on business. Sambo didn't understand English, refused all food and died of a broken heart, seemingly abandoned by his master. Alternatively, he was taken gravely ill aboard ship whilst anchored at the Point and died before any medical help could be administered. Either way he was buried in unconsecrated ground some distance from the small chapel at Sunderland.

From the grave continue on along the foreshore, for the next mile or so bordering the extensive salt marshes to end up at Potts Corner, the second cottage you come to. You can reach this either by following the path along the shoreline or along the track you come to which winds out across the marshes to end up near the cottage.

Immediately beyond the cottage turn right and walk along the lane, Carr Lane, passing a number of bungalows and the entrance to a caravan park. Stick with the lane as it winds round several bends until you reach a very sharp left hand bend. Just round this on the right is a public footpath sign to Middleton. Take this and walk along to the white stile, climb this and then follow the edge of the field on your right. Climb a further stile and then head across the pastures towards Trumley Farm. You'll see a stile through the fence about twenty yards to the left of the farm, cross this and aim for the next stile which is beside the area of infil tipping; work across this to a further stile, from which walk across the field to the ladder stile at the far side. This gives you access to the marshland road followed earlier in the walk, simply turn left and walk along it back to Overton. Pass the Globe Inn (Mitchells Beers) on your right and bear right up the road to return to The Ship Hotel.

25. NORTH LUNE: WARTON

Route: Warton – Warton Crag – Crag Foot – Jenny Brown's Point – Silverdale Green – Leighton Moss

Distance: 7 miles

Map: Sheet SD 37/47 Grange-over-Sands

Start: The Black Bull, Warton, Carnforth

Access: Warton is about seven miles north of Lancaster, just west of the A6 and M6 roads. Leave the M6 at Junction 35 and go along the motorway spur to the roundabout on the A6. Turn right here, following the Milnthorpe sign. In about two hundred yards (and before you reach the next roundabout) a narrow road on your left is signposted for Warton. Drive along this, Borwick Lane, and turn left at the end, along the village's main street, to reach the Black Bull a further quarter of a mile away. There is ample parking at the pub or at a car park up the narrow road beside the pub.

By rail you can pick up this walk at Silverdale station; this is on the Preston/Lancaster to Barrow in Furness line and has an infrequent daily service.

The Black Bull (0524 732865)

At last, a Mitchells pub, and very probably one of their oldest. No one seems quite sure how old the building is or how long it has served as a pub; the concensus is that it's certainly a lot longer than the century or so that Mitchells have been brewing and that the Fifteenth Century is a reliable guess. The white painted, three storey building is certainly a respectable age, bedecked with chimneys and dominating the tiny village square just a stones throw away from the church. One end of the main bar room is dominated by a huge brick fireplace; the fire helps light the area which is served only by a series of small, wood panelled windows, causing heavy shadows on the low, heavily beamed ceiling at this end of the pub.

A large collection of old plates and carving dishes adorns shelves around the walls whilst the bar sports a single handpump supplying Best Bitter; publicity material in the pub suggests that the dark mild and E.S.B. may also be available. The Bull has a reputation locally for the home made pies and chillies that form the substance of the bar meals, these are served each lunchtime except Mondays. The pub itself is open from 11 am to 3 pm and 6 pm to 11 pm.

Warton

The village is dominated by Warton Crag, one of the great reefs of limestone that dominate the coast at the northern end of Morecambe Bay and around the Kent estuary. Viewed from a distance the southern face of the crag is a series of giant steps leading down to the saltmarshes; the lower one has been heavily quarried but the upper ones are natural scars, reflecting the way the limestone was laid down in a warm sea three hundred million years ago. The Crag, together with the marshes and much of the limestone coast to the north west, is part of an Area of Outstanding Natural Beauty.

Warton has seen a lot of development in the past few decades and now acts largely as a commuter town for Carnforth, Lancaster and Preston. The long, winding main street and a few adjoining folds remain as a reminder of the long history of the village. Main Street is liberally dotted with old yeomans cottages and rows of tiny pebbledashed cottages whose windows alone give away their antiquity. Near the Post Office is Washington House, once home to the family which produced the first President of the newly independent American Colonies. Another politician with links to the village, by marriage, was Winston Churchill. Detailed family trees of both gentlemen are displayed in St. Oswalds Church whose solid tower was built by a member of the Washington family in the fifteenth century; much of the church is somewhat younger than this. Downhill from the church are the remains of a fourteenth century rectory, now in the care of English Heritage and open daily except Mondays.

The Walk

If you've got, or can beg or borrow, a pair of binoculars then ensure that you take them on this walk – it is probably the best one for wild birds and views in this book.

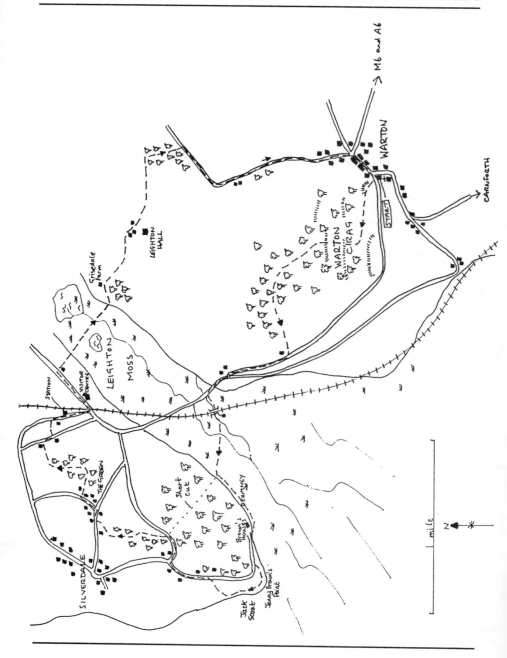

Walk up the narrow lane beside the pub, Crag Road, and angle right into the small car park a short distance up on the right. From the back of this car park walk up the rough path through the scrubby woodland to the gap stile at the top beside the information board (which outlines the attractions of the Crag area). Turn right and then left a few paces later and follow the path which takes you gradually uphill. You're walking along one of the steps along the south face of the Crag, the immense views take in the coastline for many miles to the south, the fells of the Forest of Bowland and, as you climb higher, the southern reaches of the Lake District.

Cross the stile at the top and walk ahead with the fence on your left. Look to your right for some large boulders of limestone perched on a small rise. You need to pass a few yards to the right of these and walk across the depression ahead to a large wooden stile. Beyond this scramble up the path to the next small plateau and continue to head for the highest point of the Crag. Walking to this may prove a little tricky as the area is well blessed with thorn trees and scrubby ash and the ground surface a jigsaw of limestone blocks and hollows. These are a common feature of limestone areas and reflect differential weathering of the rock, the small ridges are called clints and the fisures between known as grikes. At the right time of year these grikes will be rich with lime loving plants and flowers; Warton Crag is well known for its wildflowers and for the butterflies and moths which make use of such.

At the summit of the Crag you'll find a triangulation pillar and a wooden beacon pole. The pillar is one of thousands throughout the country upon which the Ordnance Survey base their maps, "triangulating" with neighbouring pillars to build up an accurate picture of the shape of the countryside and towns. The pillar upon which all the other ones are homed is on a Down above Portsmouth whilst all heights are based on mean (average) sea level at Newlyn Harbour in Cornwall. The summit of the Crag has been recognised as the site of an old British Hill Fort although remains are, frankly, scant.

The path you should leave the summit by goes north from a point between the pillar and the beacon pole. It's an obvious path and within fifty yards you'll come to a signpost offering a choice of route to either Coach Road, Warton or Crag Foot. Follow the Crag Foot sign and walk off gently down through the trees, largely ash with a generous sprinkling of yew and holly. Remain with the path as it winds slowly down from the summit, following the occasional directional sign for Crag Foot. In a few hundred yards you'll reach a rough, walled road known as Occupation Road. Turn left along this and walk to the end about half a mile distant, enjoying the ever increasing views across the Kent Estuary.

On reaching the end turn right and walk along down the minor road to the junction at the bottom. Go straight ahead here and then bear left and follow the main road out across the mossland. The vast, flat area to your right is Leighton Moss, one of England's premiere nature reserves, of which more later. On reaching the sharp right hand bend turn left along the track and walk along beside the drainage ditch. Pass under the railway bridge – carrying the spectacular Cumbrian Coast line which still has regular steam-hauled services during the summer – and then turn right across the solid stone bridge, essentially the sluice gate to this particular drain. Cross the gate at the far end and turn left along the embankment. Cross the stile and walk along left to a further stile, cross this and then bear right with the embankment, following it across this huge expanse of mossland, its line marked by occasional thorn trees. The area is a paradise for birdwatchers with hundreds of Oystercatcher, Dunlin, Greenshank, Curlew, Shellduck and myriad other wading birds.

At the far end of the embankment is a signpost; you should turn left towards Jenny Brown's Point. If, however, you wish to avoid this mile or so of largely coastal walk then go straight ahead with the sign towards Woodwell and walk over the hilltop to rejoin the walk later.

Having turned left follow the path along the shoreline, cross the stile and continue along towards the Point. Stick close to the shore as the area of flats and sands to your left is known, with good reason, as Quicksand Pool. On a clear day the bulk of the Forest of Bowland beyond Warton seems almost close enough to touch. Pass by the forlorn, isolated chimney (evidence, together with one passed on the other side of the moss, of the copper smelting which once took place locally) at the edge of the marshes and walk along the foreshore in front of Brown's Houses, gaining the narrow road just beyond and following this above the shoreline. In a couple of hundred yards go through the kissing gate on your left and walk onto the low headland of Jack Scout, an area of National Trust land (use the donation box at your discretion). This is a limestone knoll which offers increasingly spectacular views up into the mountains around Coniston the further round you walk. Jenny Brown's Point, named after an old woman who lived in the isolated cottages on the foreshore, is the southerly point of this knoll.

Brown's Houses and Old Smelting Chimney

Cut back inland, along the line of the wall if not before, and rejoin the minor road, turning left along this to walk past the folly-like Lindeth Tower (home, for a short time, to the celebrated Victorian novelist Mrs Gaskell) to the road junction. Turn right here up along Hollins Lane towards Carnforth. Follow this road along past the craft centre and walk up the short, steep slope into the trees. On your right you'll find a signpost directing you towards Crag Foot – this is where the short cut from the end of the embankment comes out. On your left is a sign for Woodwell; take this path, favouring the upper route, along this limestone ridge. Remain with the path through the woods, initially with a pasture to your right and a steep drop on your left, and bear gradually left with it. You should soon find yourself at a stile into a narrow pasture. Cross into this pasture, bear right and walk to the signpost on the bank top, from there following the direction indicated to The Green, essentially left. Cross the stile at the end and walk on along the edge of the woods with a wall to your right. On reaching the green door in the wall turn right and walk along the walled/fenced path. Cross the stone step stile at the end, walk along the walled track to the minor road at the end and turn right to Silverdale Green.

In about a hundred yards turn left along Bottoms Lane, towards Arnside and Milnthorpe. Just past the last house on the right take the path signposted to Burton Well and walk along this track which soon deteriorates into a walled path. Burton Well itself is in the walled inclosure off to the right at the end of this track and below the limestone cliff. You should cross the stile here and walk along to the footbridge; cross this and walk across Lambert's Meadow to the ladder stile at the woodland edge. Climb the stile and turn left, walking up the steep, stepped path into and through the woods. At the crossing of paths go straight ahead, pass beside the garage and walk to the road at the end, turning right along this.

Within fifty yards a worn footpath sign points the way, left, across the golf course. There are occasional red and white route markers but, essentially, aim to pass to the left of the two small, bare knolls but to the right of the one capped with fir trees – and beware of projectiles. Climb the stile to the left of the gate at the far side of the Course and turn right along the road, soon passing Silverdale Station on your left. A short while later turn left, cross the railway bridge and walk down to the Leighton Moss Visitor Centre.

Leighton Moss

The Visitor Centre and Leighton Moss are owned by the Royal Society for the Protection of Birds. The Moss is one of the Society's major reserves, its principal attractions are the very rare Marsh Harrier and Bittern, together with an amazing variety of migratory water birds and rare warblers. The vast area of ponds, drains and reedbeds are also home to otters whilst red squirrels and deer live in adjoining woodlands. Until 1917 the mossland was kept drained by a series of ditches and pumps and provided rich farmland, since then it has been allowed to revert to the semi-natural state you see today. The reserve is open from 9 am to 9 pm daily except Tuesdays and permits are available from the visitor centre shop; there's also a cafe here. (You don't need a permit to use the public footpath which this walk follows across the Moss).

Continue along the road away from the Visitor Centre and start to walk uphill with it. Immediately past the cottage on your right a track falls away down onto the Moss; walk down along this and out across Leighton Moss, this is the only public footpath across it. The track is thickly bordered by high reeds and bulrushes, Dogwood, Goat Willow, Spindle and Alder trees. Here and there gaps have been created offering views across the ponds and meres; about half way across is a public hide which offers uninterrupted views across the largest stretch of water. At the far end go through the gate and follow the field track along to and past Grisedale Farm, then remaining with the surfaced road to end up beside Leighton Hall. This spectacular neo-Gothic mansion was created around an old fortified manor house. It was renovated in this style by a member of the Gillow family (of the Waring and Gillow furniture company) and contains fine period furniture. The Hall is open daily during the afternoon between May and September, an additional attraction is a display of free-flying eagles and falconry on weather-suitable afternoons.

As the sign attached to the barn indicates, the public footpath cuts up the hillside to the left of the driveway leading to the Hall. Follow the line of telegraph poles up the hillside, passing to the left of the enclosure of trees half way up the slope. At the top turn right and walk along the line of trees which follow the spine of this ridgetop. The bare bones of this spine are exposed boulders and lumps of the underlying limestone. At the end climb the stile behind the green wooden fencing and follow the path through the woods to the minor road. Turn right down this and follow it all the way back to Warton village, about a mile away. Turn right at the main road to return to the Black Bull.

The River Darwen, in the Darwen Gorge – on the Riley Green walk (see pages 46 to 51)

Sample the delights of country pubs, and enjoy some of the finest walks with our expanding range of 'real ale' books:

PUB WALKS IN THE PEAK DISTRICT
– Les Lumsdon and Martin Smith

MORE **PUB WALKS IN THE PEAK DISTRICT**
– Les Lumsdon and Martin Smith

PUB WALKS IN LANCASHIRE – Neil Coates

PUB WALKS IN THE PENNINES
– Les Lumsdon and Colin Speakman

PUB WALKS IN THE LAKE DISTRICT – Neil Coates

PUB WALKS IN THE YORKSHIRE DALES – Clive Price

PUB WALKS IN THE COTSWOLDS – Laurence Main

HEREFORDSHIRE WALKS – REAL ALE AND CIDER
COUNTRY
– Les Lumsdon

PUB WALKS IN CHESHIRE – Jen Darling

There are even more books for outdoor people in our catalogue, including:

EAST CHESHIRE WALKS – Graham Beech

WEST CHESHIRE WALKS – Jen Darling

WEST PENNINE WALKS – Mike Cresswell

NEWARK AND SHERWOOD RAMBLES – Malcolm McKenzie

RAMBLES AROUND MANCHESTER – Mike Cresswell

WESTERN LAKELAND RAMBLES – Gordon Brown

WELSH WALKS: Dolgellau and the Cambrian Coast
– Laurence Main

OFF-BEAT CYCLING IN THE PEAK DISTRICT – Clive Smith

THE GREATER MANCHESTER BOUNDARY WALK –
Graham Phythian

And there's more . . .

We also publish:

Guidebooks for local towns

A guide to the pubs of 'Old Lancashire'

Spooky stories

Myths and Legends

Football books

and, under our Sigma Press banner, over 100 computer books!

All of our books are available from your local bookshop.
In case of difficulty, or to obtain our complete catalogue, please contact:

**Sigma Leisure,
1 South Oak Lane,
Wilmslow, Cheshire SK9 6AR**

Phone: 0625 - 531035 Fax: 0625 - 536800

ACCESS and VISA orders welcome!